International Macroeconomics for Business and Political Leaders

T0384288

International Macroeconomics for Business and Political Leaders explains the fundamentals of international macroeconomics in a very efficient and approachable way. It explores key macro concepts, such as growth, unemployment, inflation, interest, and exchange rates. Crucially, the text also examines how these markets are interconnected so that readers fully understand why economic, political, and social shocks to nations, including the United States, China, Germany, Japan, and Brazil, must be evaluated in the context of all three macroeconomic markets: goods and services, credit, and foreign exchange.

This book is as relevant and useful to individuals who have successfully taken and passed a Principles of Economics course, or perhaps more, as it is to those who have never taken any economics in high school or college but are motivated to understand the way international economies act and react. The text uses an innovative approach to teach supply and demand principles, without using graphs, so these tools are understandable and accessible to any interested reader or audience. This is not a theory-for-theory's-sake textbook but a practice-oriented, common-sense approach to explaining international macroeconomics, which quickly connects readers to real world events.

John E. Marthinsen is Professor of Economics and International Business at Babson College in Babson Park, MA, where he holds The Distinguished Chair in Swiss Economics. Dr. Marthinsen has extensive consulting experience, working for both domestic and international companies, as well as the U.S. government.

Routledge Focus on Economics and Finance

The fields of economics are constantly expanding and evolving. This growth presents challenges for readers trying to keep up with the latest important insights. Routledge Focus on Economics and Finance presents short books on the latest big topics, linking in with the most cutting edge economics research.

Individually, each title in the series provides coverage of a key academic topic, whilst collectively the series forms a comprehensive collection across the whole spectrum of economics.

International Macroeconomics for Business and Political Leaders

John E. Marthinsen

LONDON AND NEW YORK

First edition published 2017
by Routledge
2 Park Square, Milton Park, Abingdon, Oxon, OX14 4RN

and by Routledge
605 Third Avenue, New York, NY 10017

First issued in paperback 2021

Routledge is an imprint of the Taylor and Francis Group, an informa business

© 2017 John E. Marthinsen

British Library Cataloguing in Publication Data
A catalogue record for this book is available from the British Library

Library of Congress Cataloging in Publication Data
A catalog record for this book has been requested

ISBN 13: 978-0-367-78819-3 (pbk)
ISBN 13: 978-1-138-63538-8 (hbk)

Typeset in Times New Roman

by diacriTech, Chennai

To my sons, Eric and Nils

Contents

Figures

Preface

How should business managers and public policymakers react when a nation's interest rates, income, and foreign exchange rates all fall at once? What causes such changes, and do these economic variables always move in the same direction? For businesses that sell only in domestic markets and purchase only domestically sourced inputs, are changes in exchange rates important? What causes nations to go into recessions and unemployment to rise? Can governments or central banks do anything to help them recover? For countries experiencing strong economic growth, are there policies that can sustain it?

The goal of this short book is to provide a highly intuitive and integrative set of economic tools and concepts that can be used to answer these questions and many more. International macroeconomics may seem rather esoteric and somewhat removed from the mainstream of our daily lives, but the truth is quite the contrary, because its ebbs and flows help shape many of the choices we make. For this reason, understanding these causes, effects, and interactions is important, not only for the improvements it can make to business and political decision-making but also for many of the personal decisions and situations we confront each day.

Acknowledgements

I learned, in a very interesting way, that "necessity is the mother of invention," when I was asked to teach an executive education module on international macroeconomics to a bright group of Swiss students, who were enrolled at the University of Bern Applied Sciences and visiting Babson College for one week. The challenge for me was accomplishing this task in only eight hours – a portion of which needed to be spent on student presentations of current events. Not finding a textbook or case of sufficient brevity and depth, I wrote this book and have used it, successfully, for various executive audiences. Therefore, I wish to start by thanking Jay Rao, Professor of Innovation and Strategy at Babson College, for the invitation, which gave me the incentive to create a solution. I am also very grateful for the feedback and cooperation of Daniel Huber, Professor of Innovation Management at Bern University of Applied Sciences. Finally, I owe a large debt of gratitude to Professors Nestor Azcona, Mahdi Majbouri, and Josh Staveley-O'Carroll for their insightful and helpful feedback, as well as to Eric Marthinsen for his lucid and perceptive comments. Any mistakes rest clearly with me.

Abbreviations

Abbreviation	Term
BoP	Balance of Payments
C	Consumption: Personal Consumption Expenditures
CA	Current Account
CPI	Consumer Price Index
CR	Credit
EUR	Euro: Euro Area's Currency
EX	Exports
FA	Financial Account (in the Balance of Payments)
Fed	U.S. Federal Reserve System
FX	Foreign Exchange
G	Government Expenditures for Final Goods & Services
GDP	Gross Domestic Product
GDP-PI	GDP Price Index
G&S	Goods & Services
I	Investment: Real Business Investment
IM	Imports
IMF	International Monetary Fund
KA	Capital Account (in the Balance of Payments)
M	Money Supply
M1	Currency in Circulation + Checking Accounts
M2	M1 + Near Money

M3	M2 + Highly Liquid Financial Assets
MXN	Mexican Peso
NE	Net Exports
NEO	Net Errors and Omissions (in the Balance of Payments)
NGDP	Nominal GDP
P	Average Domestic Price Level of Final Goods and Services
P*	Average Foreign Price Level of Final Goods and Services
PCE-PI	Personal Consumption Expenditures Price Index
PPI	Producer Price Index
Q	Quantity per Period
RGDP	Real Gross Domestic Product
RRI	Reserves and Related Items (in the Balance of Payments)
USD	U.S. Dollar
V	Velocity of Money
$	United States Dollar
€	Euro
£	British Pound
¥	Japanese Yen
≡	"Is defined as being equal to" (e.g., 1 Kilometer ≡ 1,000 Meters)

1 Measures of economic health

A nation's economic health is often evaluated by its growth rate, labor market conditions, and inflation rate. Economic growth is measured by changes in real gross domestic product (RGDP). Labor market conditions are usually assessed by the unemployment rate, employment-to-population ratio, and labor force participation rate. Finally, inflation is measured by percentage changes in a nation's price index. Let's explore these economic measures, how they are calculated, and what they mean.

Gross domestic product (GDP)

Gross domestic product (GDP) measures the *market* value of all *final* goods and services (G&S) *produced* within a nation's borders during a given time period, such as a year. The italicized words in this definition deserve clarification. First, GDP measures *market* values in order to combine disparate products, such as clothing, wheat, airplanes, and computers, into a single money value. By using market values, GDP excludes underground transactions that are usually hidden from view because they are not conducted on open markets and, therefore, are difficult (if not impossible) to measure. Second, GDP counts only the value of *final* products because also including intermediate G&S (i.e., ingredients or components) would be double counting. For example, think of the double counting involved if GDP included the value of an airplane plus all its parts (e.g., steel, plastic, wheels, and seats).[1] Finally, GDP includes the value of G&S *produced*, which means products do not need to be sold to be counted.

Four ways to view GDP

GDP can be viewed in a number of helpful ways, but regardless of the approach, each of them sums to the same total (GDP) number. Mercifully, each of these approaches has a strong element of common sense, which makes all of them easy to understand.

Price-quantity approach to explaining GDP

GDP can be calculated by multiplying the price of every final good and service by the quantity produced per period and then summing these products. If P stands for the *price of final G&S* and Q stands for the *quantity produced each period*, then GDP equals the sum of all these prices times quantities (see Figure 1.1).

GDP	$\equiv$	The "$\equiv$" notation means the relationship is definitional. Therefore, there is no controversy in economics over the relationship.
GDP	$\equiv$	Sum of $(P \times Q)$

Figure 1.1 GDP: Price-quantity approach.

G&S demand approach to explaining GDP

The four major economic sectors that demand a nation's final G&S are (1) domestic consumers, (2) domestic businesses, (3) domestic governments (national, state, and local), and (4) foreign consumers, businesses, and governments. Therefore, GDP can be viewed as the sum of personal consumption expenditures (C), *intended* business investment expenditures plus *unintended* changes in business inventories (I), government expenditures on final products (G),[2] and net export (NE) expenditures.[3] See Figure 1.2.

GDP $\equiv$	Personal Consumption	+	Business Investment	+	Government Spending	+	Net Exports
GDP $\equiv$	C	+	I	+	G	+	NE

Figure 1.2 GDP: Goods & services (G&S) demand approach.

Two important points are worthwhile remembering about I. First, in the context of GDP, businesses purchases of final G&S include products, such as machinery, tools, equipment, and inventories, as well as residential housing[4] and business construction. This GDP component does not include the demand for financial investments in stocks, bills, notes, or bonds. Second, increases in business inventories can be intended (voluntary) or unintended (involuntary). Businesses voluntarily increase their inventories when they expect sales to rise. They involuntarily do so when they produce goods that are not sold. In either case, any increase in inventory quantity is counted as part of GDP's investment (I) component.

Income approach to explaining GDP

Any time a good or service is produced, someone is paid for the effort. Therefore, GDP can also be viewed as the sum of incomes earned from producing final G&S. Economists categorize income-earners into four groups, namely labor, natural resources, real (physical) capital, and entrepreneurs. The return to physical and mental capabilities of labor is called the *wage*; the return to natural resources is called *rent;* the return to real capital (i.e., human-made aids to production) is called *interest*,[5] and the return to risk-taking (entrepreneurship) is called *profit*. See Figure 1.3.

GDP	≡	Wages	+	Rent	+	Interest	+	Profits

Figure 1.3 GDP: Income approach.

Money supply-and-velocity approach to explaining GDP

In *Chapter 9: Money, banking, and central banks*, we will discuss how nations measure their money supplies. For now, think of money (M) as all the coins and paper currency that individuals in a nation hold (outside banks) plus their checking accounts. In 2016, the U.S. money supply equaled approximately $3 trillion. At the same time, U.S. GDP totaled about $18 trillion. How can a nation's GDP be so much larger than the money available to purchase it? The answer is money is spent more than once a year. In short, it has a velocity (V). Therefore, if a nation's GDP equaled $18 trillion and money supply equaled only $3 trillion, then each dollar must have been spent (for newly produced G&S) six times during the course of the year. As a result, GDP can be viewed as the product of M times V. See Figure 1.4.

GDP	≡	Money Supply	×	Velocity of Money
GDP	≡	M	×	V

Figure 1.4 GDP: Money supply-velocity (M × V) approach.

Nominal versus real GDP

The *price-quantity approach to explaining GDP*, which was described in the last section, is helpful for clarifying the difference between real and nominal GDP. Nominal GDP (NGDP) equals the sum of prices times quantities for all final G&S produced per period. Therefore, it can increase if production (i.e., Q) and/or prices (i.e., P) rise. Increases in prices give the illusion of growth and prosperity but without material substance. To eliminate this illusion, nations calculate *real* GDP (RGDP), which removes the effects of higher prices by multiplying the quantities produced each period by the prices in a base year (see Figure 1.5). By using only base-year prices, RGDP can rise only if output (i.e., Q) per period increases. In virtually all economic discussions, RGDP is more important than NGDP.

NGDP	$\equiv$	Sum of (Current Prices × Current Final Production per Period)
RGDP	$\equiv$	Sum of (Base Year Prices × Current Final Production per Period)

Figure 1.5 NGDP versus RGDP.

To maintain a contemporary perspective, national statistical offices periodically change the base year used to calculate RGDP. The new one selected is determined by its stability relative to nearby years. Figure 1.6 shows the difference between RGDP and NGDP for 2000, 2009, and 2017, assuming 2009 is the base year.

Year	NGDP	RGDP
2000	$P_{2000} \times Q_{2000}$	$P_{2009} \times Q_{2000}$
2009	$P_{2009} \times Q_{2009}$	$P_{2009} \times Q_{2009}$
2017	$P_{2017} \times Q_{2017}$	$P_{2009} \times Q_{2017}$
$NGDP \equiv P_{\text{Given Year}} \times Q_{\text{Given Year}}$		
$RGDP \equiv P_{\text{Base Year}} \times Q_{\text{Given Year}}$		

Figure 1.6 RGDP versus NGDP (2009 = base year).

Calculating a nation's economic growth rate

Economic growth is measured as a percentage change in RGDP. Just as a movement from $100 to $110 is a 10 percent change (i.e., $10/$100 = 0.10 × 100 percent = 10 percent) and a movement from $110 to $120 is a

9.1 percent change (i.e., $10/$110 = .091 \times 100$ percent $= 9.1$ percent), the percentage change in RGDP is calculated by dividing the change in RGDP by the original RGDP and then multiplying the result by 100 percent. Figure 1.7 shows the economic growth calculation between Year 1 and Year 2.

$$\text{Economic Growth} \equiv \frac{\text{RGDP}_{\text{Year 2}} - \text{RGDP}_{\text{Year 1}}}{\text{RGDP}_{\text{Year 1}}} \times 100 \text{ percent}$$

Figure 1.7 Calculating real economic growth.

Business cycles

Business cycles are "recurring, irregular, and unsystematic movements in real economic activity around a long-term trend."[6] Recessions are significant contractions in economic activity, which are spread broadly across an economy and last for more than a few months. Expansions (also called recoveries) are just the opposite.

In the news media, a nation is often said to be in a "recession" when its RGDP falls for two consecutive quarters, but, officially, recessions are not measured or dated this way. Rather, a spectrum of macroeconomic variables is used to gauge a nation's economic health. For example, the National Bureau of Economic Research, a private organization, measures and dates U.S. expansions and contractions (i.e., business cycles) by using the employment-to-population ratio (also called the employment rate), real personal income, sales volumes for the manufacturing and trade sectors, and industrial production. These variables were chosen above others because, historically, they were shown to be the most timely, significant, reliable, consistent, and accurate reflections of U.S. economic activity. RGDP is excluded from this list because it is reported relatively infrequently (quarterly, instead of monthly) and is often subject to considerable revisions.

Measures of labor market health

Three important measures of labor market health are the unemployment rate, employment-to-population ratio, and labor force participation rate. This section explains what they mean, their limitations, and how these measures complement each other.

Labor market composition

Figure 1.8 separates a nation's *total population* into a number of helpful categories. Starting from the top, individuals are classified as being either part

Unemployment Rate, Employment-to-Population Ratio, and Labor Force Participation Rate		
Total Population *300 mm*		
Civilian Non-Institutional Population 16+ *250 mm*		**Not Members of the Civilian Non- Institutional Population 16+** (Mainly juveniles, military personnel, and the incarcerated) *50 mm*
Civilian Labor Force *150 mm*		**Civilian Non-Institutional Population 16+ but Not Part of the Civilian Labor Force** (Mainly retirees, students, and discouraged workers) *100 mm*	
Employed *141 mm*	**Unemployed** *9 mm*		

Summary of labor market measures											
Unemployment Rate	≡	Unemployed / Civilian Labor Force	=	9 mm / 150 mm	=	0.06 × 100%	=	6%
Employment-to-Population Ratio	≡	Employed / Civilian Non - Institutional Population 16 +	=	141 mm / 250 mm	=	0.564 × 100%	=	56.4%
Labor Force Participation Rate	≡	Civilian Labor Force / Civilian Non - institutional Population 16 +	=	150 mm / 250 mm	=	0.60 × 100%	=	60%

Figure 1.8 Unemployment rate, employment-to-population ratio, and labor force participation rate.

or not part of the *civilian non-institutional population 16+* (i.e., 16 years or older). Those who are *not part* of the civilian non-institutional population are mainly individuals who are younger than 16 years old, in military service, or incarcerated.

The civilian non-institutional population 16+ is then separated into those individuals who are either part or not part of the *civilian labor force*. Individuals who are part of the civilian non-institutional population 16+ but not part of the civilian labor force are those who are not seeking work, such as retirees, students, and discouraged workers.

Finally, the civilian labor force is separated into those individuals who are either employed or unemployed. An *employed* individual worked for at least one hour during the survey period, which means part-time[7] and full-time workers are counted the same. To be classified as *unemployed*, the person must be jobless, able to work, *and* actively seeking employment.

Unemployment rate

A nation's unemployment rate equals the number of individuals who are unemployed divided by the civilian labor force. Given the values in Figure 1.8, the number of unemployed individuals equals 9 million and the civilian labor force equals 150 million. Therefore, the nation's unemployment rate equals 6 percent (i.e., 9 million/150 million = 0.06×100 percent = 6 percent).

What is full employment?

Due to normal frictions in an economy, there will always be individuals who are temporarily out of work, such as those moving from one job to another and graduates looking for their first employment opportunities. This type of unemployment is acceptable and part of every healthy economy. Due to this *frictional unemployment*, nations do not seek 0 percent unemployment rates. Rather, their goals are more modest, reflecting unemployment rates that would exist if the economy was growing at a normal rate and inflation was under control. Sustainability is a key to each nation's full employment goal, which is why it is often called the *natural rate of unemployment* or the *non-accelerating inflation rate of unemployment*.

Due to dissimilarities in international labor markets, especially with regard to demographics, minimum wage legislation, social welfare programs, and labor mobility, nations define their full employment targets differently. Nevertheless, if you keep in mind that a 5 percent unemployment rate is about where most countries would like to be, you are within striking distance of their full employment goals.

Just the facts about a nation's unemployment rate

Confusion and misunderstanding often arise in discussions about a nation's unemployment rate and for good reason. Did you know that:

- Only individuals who are actively seeking work are counted as *unemployed*, which means that if someone tries to find work and then gives up in frustration, the unemployment rate falls.
- Unemployment figures do not account for differences in family situations. As a result, the loss of a job by a single income earner (e.g., mother or father) in a family of four is counted the same as the loss of

job by a live-at-home high school student in a family of four, where the other three family members are fully employed.

• The unemployment rate is not adjusted for underemployment, which occurs when individuals are working in occupations below their abilities, training, or skill levels. Therefore, a down-on-his-luck Ph.D. in microbiology, who is scrubbing floors at a fast food restaurant and earning the minimum wage, is considered to be just as fully employed as a microbiologist researching a cancer cure, working at a teaching hospital, and earning a six-digit salary.

• The unemployment rate tends to lag behind economic activity. As a result, it is not a good reflection of current economic conditions. When the economy contracts, businesses are understandably reluctant to lay off talented and dedicated employees. So, the unemployment rate does not rise immediately after the economy contracts. Similarly, when the economy begins to recover from a recession, businesses are slow to rehire, and when they do, they tend to employ temporary workers, first, so they do not have to pay full-time benefits. Business managers are also reluctant to take on new workers during the early recovery stages because they need to be sure the upturn is real. Therefore, a rising economy does not immediately cause a falling unemployment rate.

Employment-to-population ratio (also called the employment rate)

The employment rate measures the number of people employed divided by the civilian non-institutional population 16+. Therefore, an unemployment rate of 6 percent does not mean the employment rate is 94 percent. In Figure 1.8, the employment rate equals 56.4 percent because the number of individuals employed equals 141 million and the civilian non-institutional population 16+ equals 250 million (i.e., 141 million/250 million = 0.564 × 100 percent = 56.4 percent).

Labor force participation rate

The labor force participation rate measures the civilian labor force divided by the civilian non-institutional population 16+ (see Figure 1.8). This measure is particularly important to nations where workers have dropped out of the labor force – often due to job discouragement and the lack of opportunities. The lower a nation's labor force participation rate compared to normal (or past) years, the higher the likelihood that the health of the economy is in jeopardy. In Figure 1.8, the labor force participation rate equals 60 percent because the civilian labor force equals 150 million and civilian non-institutional population 16+ equals 250 million (i.e., 150 million/250 million = 0.60 × 100 percent = 60 percent).

Measuring a nation's average price level and inflation rate

Average prices are measured at the macroeconomic level with price indices, and inflation rates are percentage changes in these indices. Let's begin by explaining what a price index is and, afterwards, turn our attention to the four most frequently used price indices for calculating inflation.

What is a price index?

A price index is a *unitless*, *normalized*, *weighted average* number, such as 100, 105, and 92. Let's discuss each of these italicized characteristics. *Unitless* means a price index is not denominated in any currency, such as the dollar ($), euro (€), or yen (¥). *Normalized* means every price index chooses a base year (say, 2009) and assigns it a value of 100. If prices rise between this base year and another year (say 2010), then the price index is higher than 100 by the extent to which the average price level has increased (e.g., 105). Similarly, if prices fall between the base year and the year under consideration, then the price index is lower than 100 (e.g., 92).

Weighted-average means the price index measures the importance of each price by its product's relative significance in the index. For example, the prices of oil, steel, and computers carry larger weights than clothespins, shoelaces, and belts. As will be explained below, different price indices focus on different product groups for different purposes.

GDP price index (GDP-PI)

The GDP price index (GDP-PI) measures the average price of all the final G&S produced within a nation's borders during a given time period. In short, it measures the prices of all the G&S included in a nation's GDP. Oftentimes, the GDP-PI is called the *GDP price deflator* or *implicit price index*. Because it measures only the prices of final products produced within a nation's borders, the GDP-PI excludes prices of imported final G&S, but keep in mind that the price of imported inputs (not final products) can indirectly affect a nation's GDP-PI by increasing costs of production.

Three other frequently used price indices: CPI, PCE-PI, and PPI

Besides GDP-PI, three other price indices are frequently cited and used. They are the consumer price index (CPI), personal consumption expenditure price index (PCE-PI), and producer price index (PPI).

Consumer price index (CPI)

The consumer price index (CPI) measures the average price of a fixed basket of consumption G&S. This market basket reflects spending patterns of the average domestic household. Because new products are constantly introduced and old ones abandoned, the *market basket* used to calculate this price index can become outdated, which is why it is revised and updated periodically. In contrast to the GDP-PI, the prices of imported final products are included in the CPI, and residential housing is treated as a consumption (C) item, rather than as business investment (I).

Personal consumption expenditure price index (PCE-PI)

The PCE-PI measures prices of G&S that are exclusively part of the C portion of GDP. Therefore, unlike the CPI, it does not include imports or residential housing, and its product mix varies from year to year, mainly due to changes in consumption patterns caused by shifting relative prices, tastes, and innovations. The PCE-PI is also different from the CPI because it is a quarterly, rather than monthly, measure. Therefore, PCE-PI is not as timely as the CPI. Relatively recently, policymakers at institutions, such as the U.S. Federal Reserve (also called "the Fed"), have paid increasing attention to movements of the PCE-PI and deemphasized changes in the CPI.

Producer price index (PPI)

The producer price index (PPI) measures price changes of G&S prior to their retail mark-ups, sales taxes, excise taxes, and distribution costs. Changes in import prices are not included in the PPI.

Measuring inflation and deflation rates

Inflation and deflation rates are calculated the same way as economic growth rates, but the appropriate price index is used instead of RGDP. Inflation is a sustained increase in a nation's average price level, and deflation (i.e., negative inflation) is just the opposite. Therefore, a price index movement from 100 to 110 is a 10 percent inflation rate (i.e., $10/100 = 0.10 \times 100$ percent = 10 percent), and movement from 100 to 92 is a deflation rate of 8 percent because the change is negative (i.e., $-8/100 = -0.08 \times 100$ percent = -8 percent). Inflation and deflation are calculated by dividing a price index's change by the original price index and multiplying the result by 100 percent. Figure 1.9 shows this calculation for price index changes between Year 1 and Year 2. Notice that Year 1 can be any year and not necessarily the base year.

$$\text{Inflation Rate} \equiv \frac{\text{Price Index}_{\text{Year2}} - \text{Price Index}_{\text{Year1}}}{\text{Price Index}_{\text{Year1}}} \times 100 \text{ percent}$$

Figure 1.9 Calculating the inflation rate.

Disinflation is different from inflation and deflation. It occurs when the price index rises, but the inflation rate falls. For example, an increase in the price index from 100 to 110 is a 10 percent inflation rate, but a subsequent increase from 110 to 115 is only a 4.5 percent inflation rate (i.e., 5/110 = 0.04545 × 100 percent ≅ 4.5 percent). Therefore, it is possible for the price index to rise but the inflation *rate* to fall.

Five inflation rate measures are reported frequently in the news. All of them are based on the aforementioned price indices, three reflect changes in consumers' living costs, and the remaining two are broader, measuring price changes for the economy as a whole.

Three cost-of-living measures of inflation

Fluctuations in consumers' living costs are often measured by percentage changes in the CPI and PCE-PI. These are the statistics you hear and read about most often in news reports, which is why they are referred to as *headline inflation rates*. A third cost-of-living indicator, called *core inflation*, measures percentage changes in the CPI or PCE-PI without the effects of volatile product prices, such as food and energy. You might be wondering why these two important product categories are excluded. The reason is changes in food and energy prices reflect national and/or international supply and demand conditions that are affected by factors outside the control of domestic governments and central banks. Among these external factors are weather conditions (e.g., droughts, and hurricanes), wars, boycotts, cartel restrictions, and embargoes. By removing food and energy from the inflation measure, it gives political officials and central bankers a better (more realistic) target for their policy decisions.

Wholesale-level measure of inflation

Inflation at the wholesale level is measured by the percentage change in the PPI.

National or currency area measure of inflation

Inflation at the national or currency area level is measured by the percentage change in the GDP-PI.

Inflation targets

Often, central banks or governments announce inflation rate targets that vary within narrow bands, and, thereafter, they adapt their policies to attain these goals. During the first decade and a half of the 21st century, inflation targets in developed nations, such as the United States and Japan, and currency unions, such as the European Monetary Union, were within ranges as low as 0 percent to 2 percent.

Victims of inflation and deflation

Inflation is often called a *silent robber* because it has the stealth-like ability to steal purchasing power from our paychecks without opening our wallets, thereby, making it more difficult to balance our needs (and wants) with our incomes. In general, the main effect of low-to-moderate inflation rates is to redistribute income from one group to another – especially when price changes are unexpected. To understand why, remember that inflation causes consumers to pay higher prices for the G&S they purchase, but at the same time, the companies charging these higher prices earn higher revenues. Where do these revenues go? The answer is workers earn them as wages, shareholders as dividends, businesses as retained profits, and governments as tax revenues. In general, for every victim, there is usually a beneficiary. If lenders lose, then borrowers gain. If workers lose, businesses and stockholders gain, and if governments lose, taxpayers gain. Therefore, victims of inflation are those whose incomes and/or wealth rise slower than inflation. For example:

- Lenders are harmed if the real purchasing power of the interest they earn is lower than expected.
- Employed individuals are harmed if their take-home pay rises slower than inflation because their incomes can purchase fewer G&S.
- Retired individuals are hurt if their pensions lag behind the inflation rate and/or if their assets, such as retirement savings, benefits, and possessions (e.g., precious metals, real estate, artworks, and jewelry), rise in value slower than inflation.
- Governments are put under budgetary pressures if their tax revenues rise slower than inflation and/or if their social welfare expenditures rise at rates higher than inflation.

- Businesses are hurt when competition prevents them from increasing product prices, but their input costs keep rising.
- Export industries are hurt if domestic prices rise more rapidly than the domestic currency's value falls.

Unexpected deflation also redistributes income, and its victims are just the opposite from the victims of unanticipated inflation. In particular, those harmed are mainly borrowers, who end up paying interest that has more real purchasing power than expected, retired individuals, whose asset values and pensions fall more than prices, governments, whose tax revenues are eroded, and businesses, whose prices fall faster than costs.

Does inflation or deflation hurt nations as a whole?

Because unexpected inflation and deflation mainly redistribute incomes, it is natural to ask when, if ever, they might harm the nation as a whole. In answering this question, it is important to distinguish between causes and effects. Let's consider deflation.

In *Chapter 3: Goods and services market* we will learn that a nation's price index can fall if its demand for G&S decreases or supply increases. When demand falls, a nation's growth slows or declines, which reduces prices and decreases both production and employment. Under these circumstances, falling prices were the result and not the cause of the recession. Alternatively, if falling prices are caused by an increase in supply, perhaps due to technological improvements or lower resource costs, then falling prices are accompanied by greater output and employment. As before, the decrease in average price level is the effect and not the cause of the economic expansion.

Even though price changes are usually the result of shifting supply and demand conditions, it is possible for them to be the cause. For example, when inflation is at very high rates (called hyperinflation) or deflation is substantially lower than expected, nationwide harm can be inflicted if it impairs productivity, lowers efficiency, and/or distorts important information signals that prices – especially relative prices – convey to the market. In these situations, relative prices can become contorted, causing inefficient and ineffective behavior by consumers and businesses. For example, hyperinflation often encourages speculative activities, drawing individuals out of mainstream occupations, such as banking, carpentry, farming, manufacturing, and plumbing. As production falls, there are fewer G&S available, and the nation suffers.

Conclusion

This chapter explained some of the most important measures of economic health. In terms of a nation's growth rate, it clarified why RGDP is more important than NGDP and went on to show how GDP can be viewed in four equally valid ways, namely:

- GDP $\equiv$ Sum of (P $\times$ Q),
- GDP $\equiv$ C + I + G + NE,
- GDP = Wages + Rent + Interest + Profits, and
- GDP $\equiv$ M $\times$ V.

Three measures of labor market conditions (i.e., the unemployment rate, employment rate, and labor force participation rate) were defined and some common misperceptions about these measures were dispelled. Finally, this chapter described various price indices and their accompanying inflation rates. Of them, the GDP-PI will be most important in this book.

Notes

1 If you are thinking that GDP might penalize countries that produce raw materials, such as oil for Saudi Arabia and Russia, and favor those that produce finished goods, such as Japan and Switzerland, rest assured it does not. Exported oil is counted as a final product for the countries producing it.
2 Government transfers for social welfare programs are not included in G because the government does not directly buy a final good or service. Rather, these expenditures are included in C and I when families and businesses spend the government transfers on final G&S.
3 NE equals exports minus imports. Imports must be deducted because they represent a nation's demand for foreign (not domestic) products. Exports represent foreign nations' demand for a home country's products.
4 Residential housing is counted as business investment because homeowners have the opportunity to rent their houses and make investment returns.
5 Like many words in the English language, "interest" has multiple meanings. Later in this book, we will see that it also means the *cost of credit*. Usually, its meaning is clear from the discussion's context, but caution is advised.
6 John E. Marthinsen, *Managing in a Global Economy: Demystifying International Macroeconomics: Second Edition* (Cengage Learning, 2015).
7 Workers with part-time jobs or short-term assignments are said to be part of the "gig economy."

2   Two important keys that unlock international macroeconomics

Two important insights help to make international macroeconomics much easier to understand.

- First, virtually all macroeconomic discussions center on three interconnected markets, namely the goods and services (G&S) market, foreign exchange (FX) market, and credit (CR) market. Changes in one simultaneously affect the other two, and, therefore, any analysis that considers only one or two of these markets, in isolation, is bound to be incomplete and/or incorrect.
- Second, most economic analyses in business publications, such as *The Wall Street Journal, Financial Times, The Economist*, and *Business Week*, can be understood by using the basic tools of supply and demand.

Let's review both of these foundational macroeconomic pillars.

Three interconnected macroeconomic markets

A market brings together buyers and sellers to determine prices and quantities per period. Each of the major macroeconomic markets has a different price and quantity.

- The **G&S market** connects buyers and sellers of goods and services to determine a nation's average price level and quantity of output each period. Quantity per period in this market is RGDP, and the average price level is the GDP-PI. The G&S market was the focus of *Chapter 1: Measures of economic health*, and it will also be the focus of *Chapter 3: Goods and services market* and *Chapter 4: Fiscal policy*.

- The **FX market** connects buyers and sellers of international currencies to determine exchange rates and the quantities of currencies traded each period. FX markets are the focus of *Chapter 5: Foreign exchange market*, and this international theme is carried into *Chapter 6: Balance of payments*.
- Finally, the **CR market** connects the suppliers and demanders of credit. For now, think of credit as being all the funds that can be lent, borrowed, raised through stock issues, and invested per period, and consider its price (i.e., the cost of credit) to be the interest rate. The CR market is covered in *Chapter 7: An overview of financial markets, Chapter 8: Credit market, Chapter 9: Money, banking, and central banks*, and *Chapter 10: Central bank tools and monetary policy*.

Figure 2.1 is a highly useful illustration because it portrays the G&S, FX, and CR markets as three interconnected spinning gears. Notice how it is impossible to move one gear without moving the others, and the speed and direction in which any gear moves determine the speed and direction of the others. *Chapter 11: Putting it all together* explains how these markets interact.

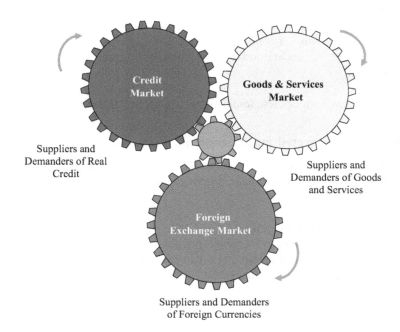

Figure 2.1 Three major macroeconomic markets.

Primer on supply and demand

Supply and demand analysis is the second major pillar of international macroeconomics. Fortunately, this economic tool is relatively easy to learn because its concepts are both logical and intuitive.

Demand: the relationship between price and quantity demanded per time period

What is the relationship between price and the quantity of a product demanded per month? Most of us understand this relationship to be inverse. If the price falls, existing customers purchase more and new consumers enter the market. If price rises, they buy less and some leave. If this relationship seems logical and intuitive, then you are well down the road toward understanding supply and demand analysis.

Supply: the relationship between price and quantity supplied per time period

What is the relationship between the price and quantity of a product supplied per month? Most of us understand this relationship to be positive, which means if the price rises, existing businesses have incentives to produce more, and other companies have an incentive to enter the market. If it falls, firms have incentives to produce less and leave. If this relationship seems logical and intuitive, then you have made it down the first leg of the supply and demand journey.

Figure 2.2 summarizes the effects that price changes have on buyers and sellers.

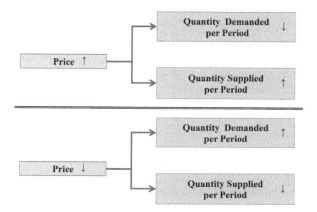

Figure 2.2 Effect of price changes on quantity demanded and supplied per period.

Consequences of changing demand

A product's price is not the only economic variable that influences buyers' decisions. There are *other* (call them "external") factors that can cause demand for a product to rise or fall, and movements in these variables cause the product's price and quantity per period to change. An increase in demand means buyers are willing and able to purchase more, which enables (and may force) suppliers to increase their prices. As a result, an increase in demand causes both price and quantity per period to rise. Similarly, a decrease in demand reduces both price and quantity per period. Figure 2.3 summarizes these causes and effects.

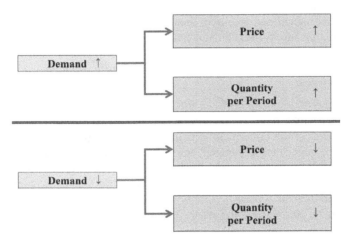

Figure 2.3 Effect of demand changes on price and quantity per period.

For now, there is no need to dwell on all the factors that cause demand to change. We will cover them in due course throughout the book, and, when we do, you will find that they have a strong foothold in common sense, and their effects are intuitive.

Primary and secondary changes in quantity per period

Prices and quantities do not change by themselves. When an external factor shifts demand, the resulting movements in price and quantity per period are *primary changes* (i.e., dominant changes). After these primary changes, the movement in price has an additional knock-on effect, which alters the quantity demanded per period. This subordinate effect on quantity is called is called a *secondary change*. Understanding the difference between primary and secondary changes is important because every primary change has a secondary change, and the primary one is the stronger of the two.

For example, suppose demand increased, causing a product's price and quantity per period to rise (see Figure 2.3 – top panel). The increased quantity is the primary effect, caused by the shift in demand. The secondary effect is the reduction in quantity demanded caused by a higher price (see Figure 2.2 – top panel). Because the primary effect is stronger than the secondary effect, higher demand results in a net increase in quantity per period (see Figure 2.4).

Primary changes in the quantity per period are due to external factors that cause movements in demand. *Secondary changes* in quantity per period are caused by movements in price.

Primary changes are stronger than secondary changes.

Figure 2.4 Primary versus secondary effects when demand changes.

Consequences of changing supply

As was the case with demand, price is not the only economic variable that influences sellers' decisions. What happens to a product's price and quantity per period when an *external* variable increases supply? An increase in supply means that firms are able to sell more at each price or willing to accept lower prices for the products they sell. As a result, an increase in supply results in more being offered to the market and at lower prices. Conversely, a decrease in the supply raises prices and decreases the quantity sold per period. Figure 2.5 summarizes these relationships.

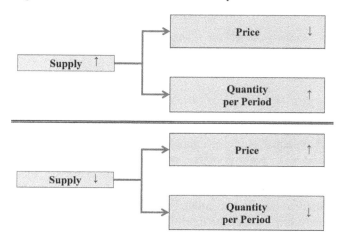

Figure 2.5 Effect of supply changes on price and quantity per period.

As was the case with demand, there is no need, yet, to list and analyze all of the major factors that cause supply to change. We will cover them, gradually, throughout the book, and, when we do, you will find that these factors and their effects reflect common sense and intuition.

Primary and secondary changes in quantity per period

Factors that increase or decrease supply cause changes in the equilibrium price and quantity per period. The initial effect that a changing external factor has on quantity per period is called a *primary change*. Afterwards, quantity per period changes, again, due to price movements. This subordinate effect is called is called a *secondary change*. As was the case with demand, understanding the difference between primary and secondary changes is important because every primary change has a secondary change, and the primary one is dominant (see Figure 2.6). For example, suppose supply increased, causing a product's price to fall and quantity per period to rise (see Figure 2.5 - top panel). The increased quantity per period is the primary effect, caused by the shift in supply. The secondary effect is the reduction in quantity supplied caused by a lower price (see Figure 2.2 - bottom panel). Because the primary effect is stronger than the secondary effect, greater supply results in a net increase in quantity per period (see Figure 2.6).

Primary changes in the quantity per period are due to external factors that cause movements in supply. *Secondary changes* in quantity per period are caused by movements in price.

Primary changes are stronger than secondary changes.

Figure 2.6 Primary and secondary effects when supply changes.

Equilibrium

Equilibrium occurs at a price where the quantity supplied and demanded per period are equal. Any price above equilibrium encourages suppliers to produce and make more available, which increases the quantity supplied, but discourages customers from buying, which decreases the quantity demanded. As a result, surpluses occur when prices are too high because more is supplied than is demanded. Fortunately, there is no need for alarm, because these surpluses create incentives for suppliers to lower their prices, and, as they do, the amount they are willing and able to produce falls, and the amounts customers are willing and able to purchase rise. When prices return to equilibrium, these incentives vanish.

By contrast, a price below equilibrium creates shortages because more is demanded than is supplied. As a result, suppliers have incentives to raise their prices, which encourage production, discourage purchases, and, thereby, reduce the shortage. Only when the price rises back to equilibrium does the shortage cease and market incentives to raise price vanish. See Figure 2.7.

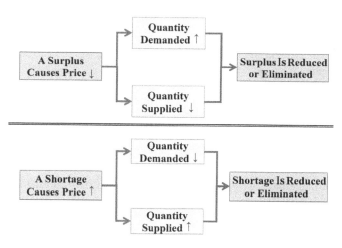

Figure 2.7 Effects of surpluses and shortages.

Consequences of changing demand and supply

What happens to price and quantity per period when demand *and* supply change simultaneously?

Demand and supply change in the same direction

As Figure 2.8 shows, if demand and supply move in the same direction, then the qualitative movement in quantity per period is always known with certainty, but the qualitative change in price is ambiguous. For example, consider what happens when both demand and supply rise. The increased demand causes price and quantity per period to rise, and the increased supply causes price to fall and quantity per period to rise. Therefore, the directional change in price depends on whether the demand adjustment is stronger or weaker than supply. By contrast, the directional change in quantity per period is strengthened by the supply and demand forces.

	Movement	Price	Quantity per Period
Demand	↑	↑	↑
Supply	↑	↓	↑
Net Change		**Uncertain**	↑
	Movement	Price	Quantity per Period
Demand	↓	↓	↓
Supply	↓	↑	↓
Net Change		**Uncertain**	↓

Figure 2.8 Effects when demand and supply shift in the same direction.

SUMMARY

• If demand and supply rise, quantity per period rises and the change in price is uncertain.
• If demand and supply fall, quantity per period falls and the change in price is uncertain.

Demand and supply change in opposite directions

Figure 2.9 shows that, if demand and supply move in opposite directions, the change in price is certain and the change in quantity is ambiguous. For example, consider what happens when demand rises and supply falls. The increased demand causes price and quantity per period to rise, and the decreased supply causes price to rise and quantity per period to fall. Therefore, the directional change in quantity depends on whether the demand adjustment is stronger or weaker than supply. The directional change in price is unequivocal (it rises!) because supply and demand movements reinforce each other (see Figure 2.9 – top panel). Similarly, if demand falls and supply rises, the price must fall, and the change in quantity per period is indeterminate (see Figure 2.9 – bottom panel).

SUMMARY

• If demand rises and supply falls, price increases and the change in quantity per period is uncertain (see Figure 2.9 – top panel).
• If demand falls and supply rises, price decreases and the change in quantity per period is uncertain (see Figure 2.9 – bottom panel).

Cause		Effects	
	Movement	Price	Quantity per Period
Demand	↑	↑	↑
Supply	↓	↑	↓
Net Change		↑	Uncertain
	Movement	Price	Quantity per Period
Demand	↓	↓	↓
Supply	↑	↓	↑
Net Change		↓	Uncertain

Figure 2.9 Effects when demand and supply shift in opposite directions.

Conclusion

This chapter introduced two fundamental pillars that are crucial to fully understanding international macroeconomics, namely, the three principal macroeconomic markets (i.e., G&S, FX, and CR markets) and basics of supply and demand analysis. Learning the principles of supply and demand can be challenging, but the results are also very rewarding. If you found this chapter to be heavy in content, you are not alone, which is why you should feel comfortable rereading it to absorb the nuances of supply and demand.

3 Goods and services market

This chapter starts by explaining how a nation's GDP-PI and RGDP are determined in the G&S market by the forces of supply and demand. Afterward, it shows how changes in these supply and demand forces cause predictable movements of the GDP-PI and RGDP.

Goods and services supply and demand

Effect price changes have the amount demanded and supplied per period

Increases in a nation's GDP-PI discourage purchases, and reductions encourage them. Therefore, the relationship between a nation's GDP-PI and RGDP is inverse. On the supply side, increases in a nation's GDP-PI encourage production, and reductions discourage it. Therefore, the relationship between the GDP-PI and G&S supplied is direct. (See Figure 3.1).

Disequilibrium

If a nation's GDP-PI is above the equilibrium level, surpluses arise, causing prices to fall, which means natural market forces should reduce or eliminate the excess. Similarly, if a nation's GDP-PI is below equilibrium, shortages occur, causing natural market forces to raise market prices.

Consequences of changing G&S demand and supply

Let's investigate what happens to a nation's GDP-PI and RGDP when G&S supply and demand change. We will start by showing the effects when only G&S demand changes, then explain the effects when only G&S supply changes, and, finally, describe the effects when both G&S demand and supply change, simultaneously.

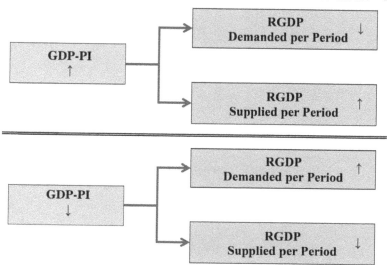

Figure 3.1 Effects a nation's GDP-PI has on RGDP demanded and supplied per period.

Consequences of G&S demand changing

Prices are not the only economic variables that influence buyers' decisions. Consumer, business, and government demands are influenced by other, external factors, such as income levels, indebtedness levels, interest rates, exchange rates, expectations, new legislation, number of buyers, investment opportunities, and wealth.

What happens to a nation's GDP-PI and RGDP if any of these *other* variables causes its G&S demand to change? For example, suppose consumer expectations improve, causing consumption (C) to rise. Businesses will realize that C has increased when their inventories start to fall and weekly production cannot keep up with orders. A natural response is for them to raise prices and produce more, in order to take advantage of the higher demand. But increasing output may not be easy. It could mean asking current employees to work extra hours, hiring additional (often, untrained) workers, and/or expanding production capacity by investing in larger facilities.

Therefore, increases in G&S demand cause the GDP-PI and RGDP to increase. Using the same reasoning in reverse, when G&S demand falls, a nation's GDP-PI and RGDP fall. Figure 3.2 summarizes these conclusions.

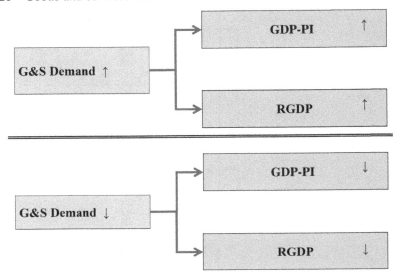

Figure 3.2 Effects G&S demand changes have on a nation's GDP-PI and
RGDP.

Consequences of G&S supply changing

As was the case with demand, price is not the only economic variable that
influences sellers' production decisions. Also important are external factors,
such as business tax rates, climate, exchange rates, expectations, immigra-
tion and emigration, input costs, natural disasters, diseases, newly discov-
ered resources, productivity, regulations, and technology.

What happens to the GDP-PI and RGDP if any of these *other* variables
causes G&S supply to rise? An increase in G&S supply means firms are
able to offer more to the market and are willing to lower their prices to do
so. Therefore, an increase in G&S supply lowers the GDP-PI and increases
RGDP. Conversely, a decrease in G&S supply raises the GDP-PI and
decreases RGDP. Figure 3.3 summarizes these relationships.

Consequences if G&S demand and supply change in the same direction

As Figure 3.4 shows, if G&S demand and supply move in the same direction,
then the qualitative movement in RGDP is always known with certainty, but
the qualitative change in GDP-PI is uncertain.

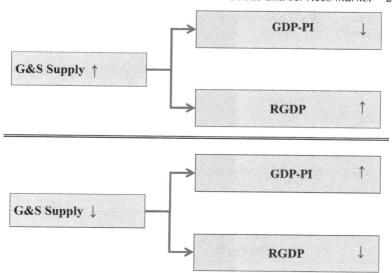

Figure 3.3 Effect G&S supply changes have on a nation's GDP-PI and RGDP.

Cause		Effects	
	Movement	GDP-PI	RGDP
G&S Demand	↑	↑	↑
G&S Supply	↑	↓	↑
Net Change		**Uncertain**	↑
	Movement	GDP-PI	RGDP
G&S Demand	↓	↓	↓
G&S Supply	↓	↑	↓
Net Change		**Uncertain**	↓

Figure 3.4 Effects when G&S demand and supply shift in the same direction.

SUMMARY

- If G&S demand and supply rise, RGDP rises and the change in the GDP-PI is uncertain (see Figure 3.4 – top panel).
- If G&S demand and supply fall, RGDP falls and the change in the GDP-PI is uncertain (see Figure 3.4 – bottom panel).

Consequences if G&S demand and supply change in opposite directions

Figure 3.5 shows that, if G&S demand and supply move in opposite directions, the qualitative change in the GDP-PI is unambiguous, and the change in RGDP is uncertain.

SUMMARY

- If G&S demand rises and supply falls, the nation's GDP-PI rises and the change in RGDP is uncertain (see Figure 3.5 – top panel).
- If G&S demand falls and supply rises, the nation's GDP-PI falls and the change in RGDP is uncertain (see Figure 3.5 – bottom panel).

Cause		*Effects*	
	Movement	**GDP-PI**	**RGDP**
G&S Demand	↑	↑	↑
G&S Supply	↓	↑	↓
Net Change		↑	**Uncertain**
	Movement	**GDP-PI**	**RGDP**
G&S Demand	↓	↓	↓
G&S Supply	↑	↓	↑
Net Change		↓	**Uncertain**

Figure 3.5 Effects when G&S demand and supply shift in opposite directions.

What causes inflation?

Inflation is caused by an increase in G&S demand and/or a decrease in G&S supply. G&S demand changes with movements in C, I, G, and NE. By contrast, changes in G&S supply are determined by shifts in the quantity and quality of a nation's resources (i.e., labor, natural resources, physical capital, and entrepreneurship), as well as other factors, such as managerial competence, technological improvements, operational efficiencies, number of sellers, and the willingness of producers to take risks.

Figure 3.6 shows that any increase in G&S demand or reduction in G&S supply causes a nation's GDP-PI to rise. A sustained increase in the GDP-PI is inflation.

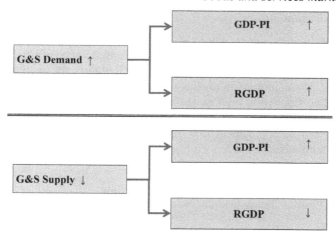

Figure 3.6 Causes of inflation.

Demand-pull inflation

Demand-pull inflation occurs when G&S demand rises (see Figure 3.6 – top panel). Notice that, along with the GDP-PI, RGDP also increases, causing the nation's unemployment rate to fall. The reduction in unemployment is a benefit to the nation, while the increase in GDP-PI is usually a disadvantage because it raises the cost of living. Figure 3.7 shows the inverse relationship between inflation and unemployment that would occur for a nation experiencing demand-pull inflation.

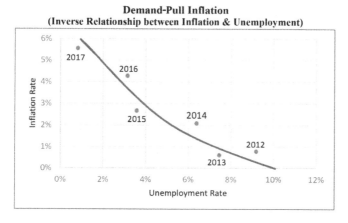

Figure 3.7 Demand-pull inflation.

Cost-push inflation

Cost-push inflation occurs when G&S supply falls (see Figure 3.6 – bottom panel). Notice that cost-push inflation has two unwelcomed effects, namely, a lower RGDP and higher inflation rate. As RGDP falls, the unemployment rate rises. The combination of rising unemployment *and* rising inflation is often called *stagflation* because the economy is *stag*nating and experiencing rising in*flation* rates. Figure 3.8 shows the positive relationship between inflation and unemployment that would occur for a nation experiencing cost-push inflation.

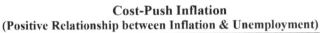

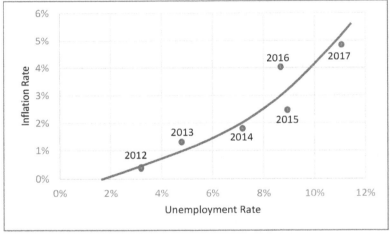

Figure 3.8   Cost-push inflation.

What causes deflation?

Deflation is a sustained decrease in prices. As Figure 3.9 shows, deflation is caused by reductions in G&S demand and/or increases in G&S supply.

Demand-side deflation

Reductions in G&S demand decrease a nation's GDP-PI and RGDP. Therefore, lower prices (or falling inflation rates) are accompanied by a rising unemployment rate (see Figure 3.9 – top panel).

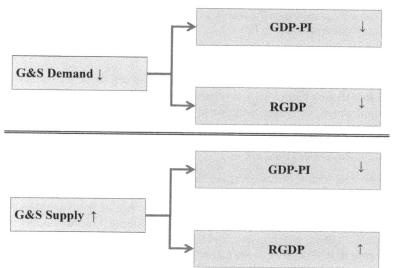

Figure 3.9 Causes of deflation.

Supply-side deflation

Increases in G&S supply cause a nation's GDP-PI to fall and RGDP to rise. Increases in RGDP tend to lower unemployment rates. For most nations, increases in G&S supply are warmly embraced and often called *Goldilocks conditions* because they are *just right*, in terms of their effect on the nation's material well-being. For nations experiencing inflation rates that are already high, increases in G&S supply may not be sufficient to cause deflation but rather may simply decrease the inflation rate (i.e., cause disinflation). Therefore, nations in the throes of rapidly rising prices may find that increases in G&S supply provide beneficial effects in terms of lower inflation *and* lower unemployment rates.

Examples

Let's review a few examples to internalize the cause-and-effect relationships when an external economic factor (i.e., a shock) hits the G&S market. You will find that using Figures 3.6 and 3.9 in connection with these examples reinforces the important G&S supply and demand relationships.

Increased government spending

An increase in G raises G&S demand (i.e., C + I + G + NE), which causes the GDP-PI and RGDP to rise (see Figure 3.6 – top panel). A rising GDP-PI puts upward pressure on the nation's inflation rate, and higher RGDP causes the unemployment rate to fall.

Decreased net exports

A decrease in NE causes G&S demand to fall, thereby reducing the GDP-PI and RGDP (see Figure 3.9 – top panel). Due to the decrease in RGDP, the unemployment rate rises, and due to the reduction in GDP-PI, downward pressure is put on the inflation rate.

Rising residential home prices

Rising real estate prices increase the wealth of homeowners across the nation. This added wealth reduces the need for households to save for retirement, which encourages families to consume more of their monthly paychecks. The increase in C raises G&S demand, putting upward pressure on a nation's GDP-PI, inflation rate, and RGDP (see Figure 3.6 – top panel). The increase in RGDP reduces the nation's unemployment rate.

Rising productivity

Rising productivity increases a nation's G&S supply, which causes the GDP-PI and/or inflation to fall and RGDP to rise. The increase in RGDP reduces the country's unemployment rate (see Figure 3.9 – bottom panel).

Conclusion

Three important concepts were introduced in this chapter. First, a nation's GDP-PI and RGDP are determined in the G&S market by the forces of supply and demand. Increases in G&S demand raise both the GDP-PI and RGDP, and decreases have the opposite effect. By contrast, changes in G&S supply cause the GDP-PI and RGDP to move in opposite directions. An increase in G&S supply causes the GDP-PI to fall and RGDP to rise, while a decrease has the opposite effect. When RGDP rises, it typically reduces the unemployment rate, and a falling RGDP normally increases it.

Second, inflation, which is a sustained increase in prices, is caused by increases in G&S demand and/or decreases in G&S supply. When inflation is caused by changes in G&S demand, it is called demand-pull inflation. When the change caused by movements in G&S supply, it is called cost-push inflation. Deflation, which is a sustained decrease in prices, is caused by reductions in G&S demand and/or increases in G&S supply. Finally, one of the beauties of market systems is their inherent stability, which means movements away from equilibrium automatically set up forces that return the nation to where RGDP supplied and demanded are equal.

4 Fiscal policy

Discretionary changes in government taxes and spending are called *fiscal policies*. They affect G&S demand through a number of channels, such as (1) amounts spent on newly produced G&S; (2) transfer payments (e.g., social welfare benefits) to households and businesses; (3) loans, such as those encouraging and supporting agriculture, innovation, entrepreneurship, education, housing, urban development, veterans, and disaster relief; and (4) changes in the tax rates that households and businesses bear. The amount and manner in which government funds are spent and tax rates are altered can strongly influence a nation's demand for G&S. Enacting responsible fiscal policies is a serious job with serious consequences, which is why it can take years to learn the discipline and even longer to master the art of providing a nation with the optimal level of government involvement.

Government deficits, surpluses, and debts

When national governments spend more than they receive in tax revenues, they usually borrow to finance these *deficits*. A deficit is measured over a period of time, such as a quarter or year, and the sum of all these deficits minus the amounts a government has repaid is called the *national debt*. Conversely, a *surplus* occurs when a government earns more than it spends. Over the course of our lifetimes, most of us try to repay all of our outstanding debts – mainly so we do not burden our relatives with them. Governments (theoretically) do not have lifetimes. As a result, it is not at all clear whether these debts must ever be repaid. Healthy and profitable corporations are not expected to reduce or pay off their debts. All they must do is service their loans by promptly paying interest, amortization, and principal obligations.

Fiscal policy and its effect on G&S demand

Recall from *Chapter 2: Goods and services market* that G&S demand equals personal consumption expenditures (C) plus business investment expenditures (I) plus government expenditures on final G&S (G) plus net export expenditures (NE). See Figure 4.1.

G&S Demand	$\equiv$	C	+	I	+	G	+	NE

Figure 4.1 Components of G&S demand.

Figure 4.2 illustrates the cause-and-effect consequences of expansionary fiscal policies. Greater G directly increases G&S demand. Reductions in personal income taxes increase C, and reductions in business tax rates increase I. As a result of these changes, G&S demand increases, causing the nation's GDP-PI and RGDP to rise. Using the same reasoning, we find that contractionary fiscal policies have just the opposite effects.

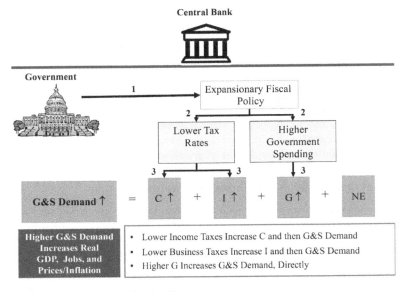

Figure 4.2 Expansionary fiscal policy.

Why do governments focus on G&S demand and not G&S supply?

Why do governments normally focus on changing the nation's G&S demand rather than supply? One reason is because demand management is easier and quicker, which is important to political leaders seeking voter support in recurring elections. Because changes in G&S supply usually take longer, meaningful supply-side policies may bear their greatest fruits long after an incumbent has lost his/her bid for reelection. To increase G&S supply, political leaders need to focus on policies that emphasize technological discoveries and innovations, entrepreneurship, human capital development, improved labor-management relations, better corporate governance practices, easier ways to form businesses, better enforcement of contracts, and informed international trade policies. They also need to consider the proper role (and limits) governments should play in the economy to ensure that efficiency and growth are not inadvertently or excessively sacrificed for redistribution purposes.

Government transfer payments, taxes, and cyclical deficits

What happens to government deficits when a nation falls into a recession or has an economic recovery? As Figure 4.3 shows, when a nation's GDP falls (and unemployment rises), automatic stabilizers are activated in the form of increased government transfer payments to finance social welfare programs, such as subsidies and unemployment compensation. In addition, tax revenues fall as existing tax rates are applied to a declining income base. Therefore, budget deficits rise automatically during recessions and fall automatically during expansions. Deficits caused by declining economic activity are called *cyclical (or passive) deficits* because they are non-discretionary,

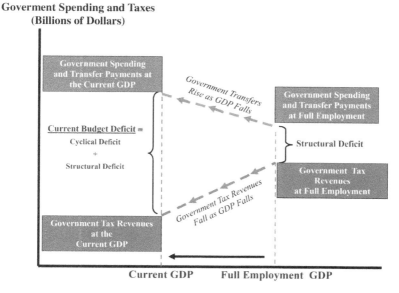

Figure 4.3 Structural and cyclical deficits.

automatic, and reflexive responses to declining economic activity. By contrast, deficits caused by discretionary changes in government spending and/or tax rate policies are called *structural (or active or full-employment) deficits*. Structural deficits (and surpluses) are estimated by taking the difference between what government spending and tax revenues would be if the nation were at full employment.

Conclusion

Fiscal policy is the practice and art of affecting economic activity by changing tax rates and government spending for final G&S. It is an important macroeconomic tool that can have beneficial or harmful effects on an economy, depending how, when, and where it is used.

5   Foreign exchange market

The foreign exchange (FX) market is enormous by any measure, with transactions amounting to approximately five trillion dollars every business day. A FX transaction occurs each time an agreement is made to convert one currency into another. The focus of this chapter is to demystify the FX market, as well as understand how supply and demand forces determine exchange rates and cause them to change.

Four different exchange rate measures

Figure 5.1 shows the four major exchange rates that are quoted and used in financial news releases, economic analyses, financial projections, and political discussions.

	Bilateral	**Effective**
Nominal	**Nominal bilateral** exchange rate measures the value of one currency relative to another.	**Nominal effective** exchange rate measures the weighted-average value of one currency relative to a basket of other currencies (usually major trading partners).
Real	**Real bilateral** exchange rate measures the value of one currency relative to another and also considers price levels in the two nations.	**Real effective** exchange rate measures the weighted-average value of one currency relative to a basket of other currencies and also considers differences in the country's price level relative to the basket countries' weighted-average price level.

Figure 5.1 Four major exchange rate measures.

Nominal bilateral exchange rate

Nominal bilateral exchange rates are what we see in newspapers, magazines, and online publications, as well as what is reported by television news anchors and quoted by banks. *Nominal* means these exchange rates do not consider price differences between the two nations. *Bilateral* means the rate compares only two currencies. Therefore, U.S. dollars per euro (USD/EUR or \$/€), euros per U.S. dollar (EUR/USD or €/\$), Mexican pesos per Norwegian krone (MXN/NOK), and Indian rupees per Malaysian ringgit (INR/MYR) are all examples of nominal bilateral exchange rates.

Appreciation versus depreciation

The currency being valued is always in the denominator (i.e., on the bottom) of a nominal bilateral exchange rate. Therefore, \$/€ is the dollar price of a euro, €/\$ is the euro price of a dollar, and ¥/£ is the yen price of a pound. An *appreciation* means the denominator currency's value has increased, and a *depreciation* means it has fallen. Because currencies are denominated in terms of each other, an appreciation of Currency A relative to Currency B implies a depreciation of Currency B in terms of Currency A. For example, when the value of the euro depreciates from \$2 (i.e., \$2/€) to \$1 (i.e., \$1/€), the value of the dollar appreciates from €0.5 (i.e., €0.5/\$) to €1 (i.e., €1/\$).

Real bilateral exchange rate

Exchange rates are similar to other economic measures, such as GDP, in the sense that they can be stated in nominal and real terms. Most insightful economic analyses are conducted in terms of real exchange rates and not nominal ones.

A real bilateral exchange rate considers three important economic variables, which are the (1) nominal bilateral exchange rate, (2) average price level in Nation A, and (3) average price level in Nation B. An example using the United States (Nation A) and Mexico (Nation B) might help explain this measure. Suppose the price of a metric ton of wheat was USD 300 in the United States and MXN 4,500 in Mexico. At the same time, assume the Mexican peso value of the U.S. dollar was MXN 15/USD. Given these conditions, the price of wheat in both countries would be the same. To purchase U.S. wheat, Mexican peso holders would need to spend MXN 4,500 (see Figure 5.2), which is the same price they would pay at home.

$$\text{USD } 300 \times \frac{\text{MXN } 15}{\text{USD } 1} = \text{MXN } 4{,}500$$

Figure 5.2 Cost of U.S. wheat in Mexican pesos at MXN 15 = USD 1.

Similarly, for U.S. dollar holders to purchase Mexican wheat, it would cost them $300 (see Figure 5.3), which is the same price they would pay at home.

$$\text{MXN } 4{,}500 \times \frac{\text{USD } 1}{\text{MXN } 15} = \text{USD } 300$$

Figure 5.3 Cost of Mexican wheat in U.S. dollars at USD 1 = MXN 15.

If the dollar appreciated to 16 pesos (i.e., MXN 16/USD), then it would be cheaper for U.S. dollar holders to purchase wheat in Mexico and less expensive for Mexican peso holders to purchase wheat at home. The dollar cost of a metric ton of wheat in Mexico would be $281.25 (see Figure 5.4), which is lower than the $300 price in the United States.

$$\text{MXN } 4{,}500 \times \frac{\text{USD } 1}{\text{MXN } 16} = \text{USD } 281.25$$

Figure 5.4 Cost of Mexican wheat in U.S. dollars at USD 1 = MXN 16.

Similarly, the peso cost of a metric ton of wheat in the United States would be MXN 4,800, which is higher than the MXN 4,500 cost in Mexico (see Figure 5.5).

$$\text{USD } 300 \times \frac{\text{MXN } 16}{\text{USD } 1} = \text{MXN } 4{,}800$$

Figure 5.5 Cost of Mexican wheat in Mexican pesos at MXN 16 = USD 1.

Figure 5.6 shows the real bilateral exchange rate for Nation A relative to Nation B. If this rate equals one, then average prices in the two nations are the same. If it is greater than one, then the average price level in Nation A is higher than in Nation B, and if it is less than one, the reverse is true. Only if this rate changes does one country gain or lose competitive advantage relative to the other. The next section explores this issue more deeply.

Real Bilateral Exchange Rate for Nation A $\equiv$ $(FX_{B/A} \times PI_A) / PI_B$

Where,
$\quad FX_{B/A} \equiv$ Nominal bilateral value of Currency A in terms of Currency B
$\quad PI_A \equiv$ Price Index in Nation A
$\quad PI_B \equiv$ Price Index in Nation B

Figure 5.6 Real bilateral exchange rate for Nation A.

Changes in the real bilateral exchange rate

Usually, people are more interested in the *direction* and *change* of an exchange rate than they are its *level* at a particular point in time. Therefore, economic discussions tend to focus on (1) *changes* in the nominal bilateral exchange rate (rather than its level), (2) the *inflation* rate in Nation A (rather than its average price level), and (3) the *inflation* rate in Nation B (rather than its average price level).

Nation A gains competitive advantages only when its real bilateral exchange rate changes so that the all-in costs of its G&S fall relative to Nation B. This occurs when the percentage change in Nation A's currency plus Nation A's inflation rate minus Nation B's inflation rate is less than zero.[1] Figure 5.7 summarizes this relationship.

% Change in Currency A's Real Bilateral Value	$\cong$	% Change in Currency A's Nominal Bilateral Value	$+$	Nation A's Inflation Rate	$-$	Nation B's Inflation Rate

Figure 5.7 Percentage change in Nation A's real bilateral exchange rate.

An example using the United States (i.e., Nation A) and Mexico (i.e., Nation B) will help to clarify this point. Suppose the U.S. dollar depreciated by 10 percent relative to the Mexican peso, which made all U.S. G&S 10 percent cheaper for Mexican buyers. Any benefit this depreciation might bring to U.S. exporters would be offset if the: (1) U.S. GDP-PI rose by 10 percent, (2) Mexican GDP-PI fell by 10 percent, or (3) U.S. GDP-PI and Mexican GDP-PI changed in combination to offset the 10 percent U.S. dollar depreciation. Figure 5.8 summarizes these results. Notice how the U.S. dollar's real exchange rate remains unchanged despite a 10 percent depreciation of the dollar's nominal bilateral value relative to the Mexican peso. For the United States to become more competitive, the percentage change in this real bilateral exchange rate needs to be negative.

% Change in Dollar's Real Bilateral Value	=	% Change in the Dollar's Nominal Bilateral Value	+	% Change in the U.S. Price Level	−	% Change in the Mexican Price Level
0	=	−10	+	10	−	0
0	=	−10	+	0	−	−10
0	=	−10	+	2	−	−8
0	=	−10	+	−2	−	−12

Figure 5.8 10 percent depreciation of the dollar's nominal bilateral exchange rate relative to the Mexican peso without a change in the dollar's real bilateral value.

Nominal effective and real effective exchange rates

An *effective* exchange rate measures a currency's value relative to a basket of foreign currencies – usually those of major trading partners. These rates can be stated in nominal and real terms, and, of the two, the real effective exchange rate is usually more meaningful than its nominal counterpart.

Nominal effective exchange rate

Nominal effective exchange rates are index numbers. An increase in this index number for Nation A means its currency has appreciated (become more expensive) relative to major trading partners, and a decrease means its currency has depreciated (become less expensive) relative to this basket of trading partner currencies.

Real effective exchange rate

A *real effective* exchange rate measures the combination of (1) Nation A's nominal effective exchange rate relative to its major trading partners, times (2) Nation A's price index, divided by (3) a weighted-average price index for nations in the currency basket. See Figure 5.9.

Real Effective Exchange Rate

$$\frac{(\text{Nation A's Nominal Effective Exchange Rate}) \times (\text{Nation A's Price Index})}{\text{Weighted Average Price Index for Nation A's Major Trading Partners}}$$

Figure 5.9 Nation A's real effective exchange rate.

Figure 5.10 uses the United States as Nation A to provide a better picture of the real effective exchange rate.

$$\text{Real Effective Exchange Rate for U.S. Dollar} \equiv \frac{(\text{U.S. Dollar's Nominal Effective Exchange Rate})^* \times (\text{U.S. Price Index})}{\text{Weighted Average Price Index for U.S.'s Major Trading Partners}}$$

$$\equiv \frac{\text{Average Price of U.S. Products Stated in Foreign Currency Prices}}{\text{Average Price of Foreign Products Stated in Foreign Currency Prices}}$$

Remember: The U.S. dollar's value is stated in FX/$ terms, such as €/$, £/$, and ¥/$.

Figure 5.10 U.S. real effective exchange rate.

In Figure 5.10, a declining real effective exchange rate means U.S. prices (after being adjusted for exchange rates) have fallen relative to prices in foreign nations. As a result, the volume of U.S. exports should rise and imports should fall. By contrast, a rising real effective exchange rate means just the opposite, namely, the United States is becoming less price competitive relative to its major trading partners.

Figure 5.11 shows a useful formula for converting the real effective exchange rate into an approximate rate of change.[2]

$$\%\Delta \ Real \ Effective \ Exchange \ Rate \cong \%\Delta \ FX_{*/A} + \%\Delta PI_A - \%\Delta PI*$$

Where,
$\%\Delta FX_{*/A} \equiv$ Percentage Change in the Nominal Effective Value of Nation A's Currency (e.g., U.S. Dollar)
$\%\Delta PI_A \equiv$ Inflation Rate in Nation A (e.g., United States)
$\%\Delta PI* \equiv$ Average Inflation Rate of Nation A's Major Trading Partners (e.g., Major U.S. Trading Partners)

Figure 5.11 Percentage change in Nation A's real effective exchange rate.

The Bank for International Settlements (BIS), International Monetary Fund (IMF), and Organization for Economic Cooperation and Development quote real effective exchange rates for a wide range of countries. The BIS's *narrow* and *broad* indices include 26 and 51 currencies, respectively.[3]

Determining a nation's exchange rate and quantity of currency traded per period

The FX market is activated every time one currency is converted into another by households, businesses, governments, and/or central banks. The main artery for doing so is the banking system. For example, consider the U.S. dollar FX market.

Major sources of dollar demand in the FX market

The major sources of demand for U.S. dollars, are by (1) foreign individuals and businesses that import U.S. G&S; (2) investors and speculators who convert their foreign currencies into U.S. dollars to purchase dollar-denominated real and/or financial assets; (3) U.S. investors, speculators, and businesses that earn foreign currencies and convert them into U.S. dollars; (4) central banks (U.S. and foreign) that own foreign currencies and purchase U.S. dollars; and (5) individuals, businesses, and governments that demand dollars with foreign currencies to make dollar-denominated remittances (i.e., gifts, aid, and transfers).

Major sources of dollar supply in the FX market

Once the major sources of demand for a currency, like the U.S. dollar, are understood, it is relatively easy to grasp the major sources of supply, because the act of demanding one currency is the act of supplying another. Let's see why.

Most foreign exchange transactions are conducted through banks. Therefore, when a U.S. dollar holder (say, John Dollarman) purchases pounds, he is both demanding pounds from the bank and supplying dollars to it. The bank is acting as an intermediary. On the other side of this transaction might be an English resident (say, Margaret Poundstone) who is purchasing dollars with pounds. Therefore, Margaret Poundstone is supplying pounds to the bank and demanding dollars from it, while John Dollarman is demanding pounds and supplying dollars.

With this in mind, let's review the major sources of dollars supplied to the dollar-pound FX market.

- U.S. importers who purchase English G&S supply dollars to the FX market (and demand pounds).
- U.S. investors and speculators who purchase pound-denominated financial instruments supply dollars (and demand pounds).
- Investors, speculators, and businesses that earn U.S. dollar returns but want pounds supply dollars to the FX market (and demand pounds).
- The Fed, English central bank (Bank of England), or other foreign central banks that own U.S. dollars, can depreciate the dollar's value by supplying them to the FX market (and demanding pounds).
- Finally, individuals, businesses, and governments that own U.S. dollars and wish to make pound-denominated remittances supply dollars to the FX market (and demand pounds).

Effect nominal exchange rate changes have on currency demanded and supplied

A primary factor influencing the amount of currency demanded and supplied is the nominal exchange rate. For example, an appreciating dollar makes U.S. G&S more expensive to foreigners and, therefore, reduces the amount they purchase. At the same time, an appreciating U.S. dollar makes foreign G&S less expensive to U.S. residents, which increases the incentive to supply dollars to the FX market in order to buy foreign currencies and, afterwards, the products they can purchase (see Figure 5.12 – top panel). A currency depreciation has the opposite effects (see Figure 5.12 – bottom panel).

Consequences of changing currency demand

Nominal exchange rates are not the only economic factors that influence foreign currency buyers' decisions. Also important are other, external variables, such as relative changes in international central bank intervention, expectations, foreign exchange controls, prices, RGDP growth rates, real (i.e., inflation-adjusted) interest rates (also called the real cost of credit), risks, tariffs, quotas, and tax rates. If any of these *other* variables change the demand for a currency, what will happen to the nominal exchange rate and quantity of currency per period?

We know from earlier chapters that any increase in demand causes the price and quantity per period to rise. In the FX market, *price* is the

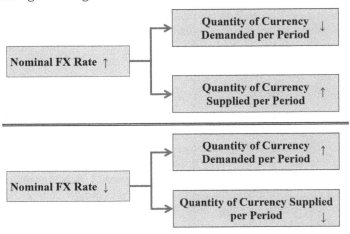

Figure 5.12 Effect of nominal exchange rate changes on the quantity of a currency demanded and supplied.

nominal exchange rate and *quantity* is the amount of currency traded per period. Therefore, an increase in the demand for a currency raises both the nominal exchange rate and quantity of currency traded per period. Reductions in currency demand have exactly the opposite effect, causing the nominal exchange rate and quantity of currency traded per period to fall. See Figure 5.13.

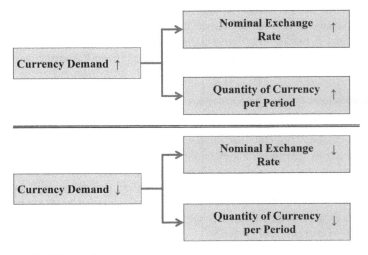

Figure 5.13 Effects of currency demand changes.

Consequences of changing currency supply

As was the case with currency demand, changes in the nominal exchange rate are not the only economic factors influencing the decisions of currency suppliers. Also important are other, external variables, such as relative changes in international central bank intervention, expectations, foreign exchange controls, prices, RGDP growth rates, real credit costs, risks, tariffs, quotas, and tax rates. Notice that these factors are the same ones that influence the demand for a currency, which should make intuitive sense because the act of demanding one currency is simultaneously the act of supplying another.

In the FX market, an increase in currency supply causes the nominal exchange rate to fall and quantity of currency traded per period to rise (See Figure 5.14 – top panel). Reductions in currency supply have exactly the opposite effect, causing the nominal exchange rate to rise and quantity of currency traded per period to fall (see Figure 5.14 – bottom panel).

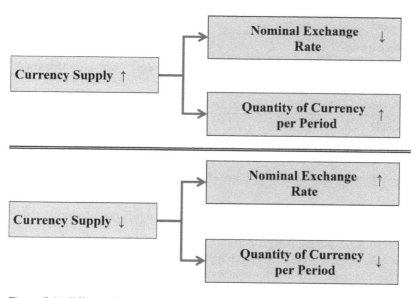

Figure 5.14 Effects of currency supply changes.

Consequences of changing currency demand and supply

What happens to the nominal exchange rate and quantity of currency traded per period when demand *and* supply change simultaneously?

Currency demand and supply change in the same direction

Figure 5.15 summarizes the effects when FX demand and supply move in the same direction. The qualitative movement in quantity per period is unambiguous, but the change in price is ambiguous. For example, if a currency's demand and supply increase simultaneously, the quantity traded per period must rise, but the change in nominal exchange rate depends on the intensity of the relative changes in supply and demand (see Figure 5.15 – top panel). Conversely, when currency demand and supply fall, the quantity traded per period must fall, but the change in nominal exchange rate is uncertain (see Figure 5.15 – bottom panel).

Cause		*Effects*	
	Movement	**Nominal Exchange Rate**	**Currency Quantity per Period**
Demand	↑	↑	↑
Supply	↑	↓	↑
Net Change		Uncertain	↑
	Movement	**Nominal Exchange Rate**	**Currency Quantity per Period**
Demand	↓	↓	↓
Supply	↓	↑	↓
Net Change		Uncertain	↓

Figure 5.15 Effects when currency demand and supply shift in the same direction.

Currency demand and supply change in opposite directions

By contrast, what happens if currency supply and demand change in opposite directions? Figure 5.16 (top panel) shows that an increase in currency demand causes both the nominal exchange rate and currency traded per period to rise. A decrease in currency supply causes the nominal exchange rate to rise and the currency quantity per period to fall. Therefore, when currency demand rises and currency supply falls, the nominal exchange rate must rise, and the change in currency quantity per period is uncertain. Conversely, when currency demand falls and currency supply rises, the nominal exchange rate must fall, and the change in currency quantity per period is uncertain (see Figure 5.16 – bottom panel).

Cause		Effects	
	Movement	Price	Quantity per Period
Demand	↑	↑	↑
Supply	↓	↑	↓
Net Change		↑	**Uncertain**
	Movement	Price	Quantity per Period
Demand	↓	↓	↓
Supply	↑	↓	↑
Net Change		↓	**Uncertain**

Figure 5.16 Effects when currency demand and supply shift in opposite directions.

Examples

Let's review a few examples to internalize the cause-and-effect relationships between economic shocks that cause shifts in supply and/or demand and, subsequently, cause changes in nominal exchange rates and the quantity of currency traded per period.

U.S. inflation falls relative to England

A decrease in the U.S. inflation rate relative to England makes U.S. G&S less expensive relative to English products and causes England's demand for U.S. products to rise. An increase in demand for U.S. G&S causes the demand for U.S. dollars to rise and its value to appreciate. At the same time, relatively lower U.S. inflation causes English products to become less attractive to U.S. residents, causing the U.S. demand for English products and the English pound to fall. When the demand for the English pound falls, the supply of U.S. dollars to the FX market falls, causing the U.S. dollar's value to appreciate. These relationships are summarized in Figure 5.16 (top panel). Notice that the change in currency quantity per period is uncertain.

Real U.S. growth rate increases relative to Japan

An increase in U.S. GDP raises household incomes, causing the demand for foreign G&S to rise. Increased U.S. purchases of Japanese products raise the demand for the yen. As a result, the supply of dollars to the FX market rises and the U.S. dollar's value depreciates relative to the Japanese yen (see Figure 5.14 – top panel).

Federal Reserve intervenes in the FX market to raise the dollar's value

Suppose the U.S. Federal Reserve intervenes in the FX market by demanding dollars with its official euro reserves. As a result, the U.S. dollar would appreciate, which means the euro would depreciate, and the quantity of dollars traded per period would increase (see Figure 5.13 – top panel).

Middle East instability causes a flight to safety in Swiss assets

Suppose turmoil in the Middle East increases economic, political, and/or social risks, causing investors to seek shelter in safe Swiss financial assets. These financial flows would increase the demand for Swiss francs and appreciate its value (see Figure 5.13 – top panel). At the same time, the demand for Middle East investments by Swiss franc holders would fall, decreasing the demand for Middle Eastern currencies and, therefore, decreasing the supply of Swiss francs to the FX market. As a result of the falling supply, the Swiss franc's value would rise and the amount of currency traded per period would fall (see Figure 5.14 - bottom panel) Together, the increase in demand and decrease in supply would cause the Swiss franc's value to rise. The change in quantity per period would be uncertain (see Figure 5.16 – top panel).

Conclusion

Understanding FX market dynamics is important for virtually everyone, even those who feel they are immune from foreign influences. For example, consider ABC Inc., a U.S.-based company that sells exclusively to domestic customers and sources its inputs solely from domestic suppliers. Just because ABC Inc. restricts its operations to the domestic market does not mean that competitors will do the same. Therefore, exchange rate movements open and close opportunities for foreign companies to compete against ABC Inc. in its domestic market, just as they open and close opportunities for ABC Inc.'s domestic competitors to do the same. For example, as the U.S. dollar appreciates, the price of foreign imports to U.S. residents falls, which could reduce the demand for ABC Inc.'s products. Similarly, if ABC's domestic competitors source their inputs internationally, an appreciated dollar would reduce the effective cost of these foreign-sourced inputs, increase domestic competitors' profits, and allow them to compete more effectively against ABC Inc.

Notes

1 Notice that this relationship is an approximation that works best when these changes are small.
2 Notice that this relationship is an approximation that works best when these changes are small.
3 See Bank for International Settlements, *The New BIS Effective Exchange Rate Indices*, www.bis.org/publ/qtrpdf/r_qt0603e.pdf (accessed October 11, 2016).

6   Balance of payments

A balance of payments (BoP) statement measures the flow of economic transactions between residents of one country and residents of the rest of the world during a given time period, such as a month, quarter, or year. Because it measures *all* international economic transactions made by a country's residents, and not just those for which one currency is converted into another, the BoP is not a pure reflection of supply and demand forces in the FX market. Examples of international transactions for which no exchange of currencies occurs are exports and imports of G&S sold on credit, domestic currency loans made to foreign borrowers, international barter transactions, and gifts-in-kind to foreign residents.

Individual countries are free to report their balance of payments figures using the definitions and collection methods they wish. For this reason, many business leaders, politicians, and academics, who use BoP reports for commercial, financial, public policy, and analytical purposes, often turn to the IMF for globally comparable figures. IMF statements are also attractive because the Fund's guidelines for data collection procedures and account presentations are usually adopted by its member nations. This chapter explains the BoP, using the IMF's presentation style and methodology.[1]

Major parts of a nation's balance of payments

Figure 6.1 shows the five major parts of a BoP statement, namely, the current account (CA), capital account (KA), financial account (FA), net errors and omissions (NEO), and reserves and related items (RRI).

Current account (CA)

CA measures a country's net earnings from (1) exports and imports of G&S, (2) primary income, and (3) secondary income. *Primary income* includes, mainly, net international earnings on labor that is contributed

Current Account	Net Earnings
Net Exports of Goods	Net Earnings
Net Exports of Services	Net Earnings
Primary Income	Net Earnings
Secondary Income	Net Earnings
Capital Account (KA)	Net Earnings
Financial Account (FA)	Net Increase in Investments Abroad
Direct Investments	Net Increase in Investments Abroad
Portfolio Investments	Net Increase in Investments Abroad
Financial Derivatives	Net Increase in Investments Abroad
Other Investments	Net Increase in Investments Abroad
Net Errors and Omissions (NEO)	A Plug Number That Ensures CA + KA + NEO ≡ FA + RRI
Reserves and Related Items (RRI)	Net Increase in Official Reserves

Figure 6.1 Balance of payments (BoP) statement.

to the production process, reinvested corporate profits,[2] interest and dividends on financial (portfolio) investments,[3] and income from renting natural resources. By contrast, *secondary income* captures international redistributions of income via transfers, aid, and gifts (i.e., remittances). Because changes in CA are perceived (often, falsely) to have close links to job creation and destruction, this account is the center of many heated disputes. If earnings from these transactions exceed expenditures, CA is positive.

Capital account (KA)

KA includes an unexpected assortment of international transactions – *unexpected* because they are not what most people think of as "capital." Included are debt forgiveness, exchanges of ownership rights to natural resources, and transfers of legal and societal creations, such as contracts, leases, licenses, and marketing assets, including goodwill. Due to its diminutive size for most nations, changes in KA are usually not major focuses of attention. When earnings from KA exceed expenditures, KA is positive.

Financial account (FA)

FA reflects a nation's international borrowing and investment/lending activities. A positive FA means the nation's residents were net international investors/lenders during the time period reported. A negative FA means that domestic individuals, businesses, and governments were net international borrowers or, alternatively stated, net recipients of foreign investments.[4]

FA is separated into major four parts: *direct investments*, *portfolio investments*, *financial derivatives*, and *other investments*.

- *Direct investments* include net changes in a nation's holdings of foreign equity, investment fund shares,[5] and debt instruments. Examples of direct investments are international mergers, acquisitions, divestitures, greenfield divestitures, greenfield investments, expansions and contractions of existing facilities, and reinvested earnings.
- *Portfolio investments*, as they appear in the BoP, seem to be just like direct investments, with subcategories that include international holdings of equity, investment fund shares, and debt instruments. Unlike direct investments, portfolio investments focus on financial transactions that do not represent controlling interests in international companies. Examples are international loans and changes in the ownership of financial securities.
- *Financial derivatives* include net changes in the market value of international transactions in options, forwards, futures, and swaps. The values of these contracts are treated separately from the items that underlie them.
- *Other investments* include changes in international bank deposits, trade credits, advances, and loans.

Reserves and related items (RRI)

RRI includes *changes in* a nation's official international reserves, which are assets a nation's central bank and/or government authority can use to purchase its domestic currency in the foreign exchange markets.[6] These assets mainly consist of central bank or government holdings of convertible foreign currencies, securities denominated in foreign currencies, gold (called "monetary gold") and other precious metals, special drawing rights (SDRs),[7] the nation's IMF reserve position, and borrowing rights from other central banks. By purchasing its own currency with these reserves, a central bank can raise its FX value or reduce the currency's rate of depreciation.

A positive[8] RRI means the nation's central bank increased its holdings of international reserves and was a net international investor/lender during the time period considered. Conversely, a negative RRI means official reserves fell, and, therefore, the central bank was a net international borrower.[9]

Balance of payments identity: $CA + KA \equiv FA + RRI$

A useful fact about BoP statements is, *if all international transactions were properly recorded,* CA + KA *must equal* FA + RRI (see Figure 6.2). We call this relationship the *BoP identity* and know it is true because any nation that spends internationally more than it earns (i.e., CA + KA is negative) must be a net international borrower (i.e., FA + RRI is negative). Likewise, any nation that earns internationally more than it spends (i.e., CA + KA is positive) must be a net international lender (i.e., FA + RRI is positive).

$$CA + KA \equiv FA + RRI$$

Figure 6.2 Balance of payments (BoP) identity in theory.

To better understand the BoP identity, suppose England imported more than it exported, causing CA + KA to equal −£200 million. To finance this gap, the nation's residents would need to borrow internationally. If the deficit was financed by individuals, businesses, and governments (i.e., by *non-central* bank entities), then FA would equal −£200 million. By contrast, if this financing gap was filled by the Bank of England (i.e., the central bank), its holdings of international reserves would fall, causing RRI to equal −£200 million.

Net errors and omissions (NEO)

The BoP identity is valid so long as all international transactions are accurately identified and measured. In practice, understandable imbalances occur due to data collection problems, caused mainly by accidentally misreported figures, incomplete information, illegal transactions that were not reported, and measurement errors. Therefore, NEO (often called *Statistical Discrepancy*) is a plug number that is added to or subtracted from CA + KA to ensure that (CA + KA + NEO) $\equiv$ (FA + RRI). As a result, the BoP identity can be more accurately defined as (CA + KA + NEO) $\equiv$ (FA + RRI) – see Figure 6.3.

$$CA + KA + NEO \equiv FA + RRI$$

Figure 6.3 Balance of payments (BoP) identity in practice.

Examples

A couple of examples will help to cement our understanding of the BoP identity.

Argentina's instability causes a flight-to-safety

Suppose political turmoil sparks financial flight from the Argentine pesos to U.S. dollars. From the U.S. perspective, these financial inflows are foreign loans, making the United States a net international borrower and causing FA to become negative (or less positive). These financial flows increase the demand for U.S. dollars, which raises the currency's value, causing exports to fall, imports to rise, and CA to become negative (or less positive). Therefore, this flight-to-safety from Argentina to the United States creates forces that cause CA to equal FA and, therefore, (CA + KA + NEO) to equal (FA + RRI).

If the U.S. Fed intervened to prevent the U.S. dollar from appreciating, a different result would occur. Without a change in exchange rate, there would be no pressure on CA to move into deficit. Rather, RRI would move into surplus because the Fed would need to sell U.S. dollars to purchase Argentine pesos. These pesos would then be part of the Fed's international reserves, causing RRI to become positive. Therefore, the positive change in RRI would equal the negative change in FA, thereby making (CA + KA + NEO) = (FA + RRI).

U.S. inflation rises relative to Mexico

Suppose U.S. inflation increased relative to Mexico, making U.S. G&S relatively less attractive. As a result, Mexico's demand for U.S. exports would fall, and the U.S. demand for Mexican imports would rise, causing the U.S. CA to become negative. To finance the resulting deficit, suppose U.S. importers borrowed pesos in the private international credit markets. FA would become negative, thereby causing the change in CA to equal the change in FA. As a result, (CA + KA + NEO) would equal (FA + RRI).

Alternatively, U.S. importers could borrow dollars (domestically) and convert them into pesos. If the Fed intervened to supply these pesos from its reserves, the importers' demand for pesos and the Fed's supply would be equal and offsetting. As a result, the Fed's international reserves would fall, causing RRI to be negative and equal to CA. Therefore, (CA + KA + NEO) would equal (FA + RRI).

Conclusion

A BoP statement measures all economic transactions between the residents of one nation and residents of the rest of the world during a given time period. Transactions and their values are separated into five broad categories, namely CA, KA, FA, NEO, and RRI. The BoP identity assures us that, if all international transitions were properly measured, (CA + KA) must equal (FA + RRI). Due to the high likelihood that measurement errors will occur, the BoP identity is better stated as (CA + KA + NEO) must equal (FA + RRI). We will find in *Chapter 10: Central bank tools and monetary policy* that a nation's monetary base changes whenever the central bank increases or decreases its quantity of official reserves.

Notes

1 In 2013, the IMF tried to make its BoP statements more transparent and user-friendly by publishing new guidelines in its *Balance of Payments and International Investment Position Manual: Sixth Edition* (BPM6). The Fund's old *Balance of Payments Manual*, which was released in 1993 and called "BPM5," was logical and easy to follow for those familiar with accounting principles. Even though the adoption by member nations has been relatively slow, the IMF has been determined to move forward with BPM6 as its lingua franca. For those readers interested in how to translate BPM5 into BPM6 and vice versa, please e-mail me at marthinsen@babson.edu for a copy of my brief monograph entitled *A Rosetta Stone for Translating BPM5 into BPM6 and Vice Versa*.
2 Reinvested corporate profits are also counted as "direct investments" if 10 percent or more of the company is foreign-owned.
3 Capital gains are not included.
4 Readers (especially those familiar with BPM5) should beware of the signs attached to FA transactions because they are the opposite of BPM5.
5 *Investment fund shares* are tradable securities issued by investment funds.
6 It is important to remember that *official reserves* are owned by central banks and not by financial institutions. In *Chapter 9: Money, banking, and central banks*, we will learn that *bank reserves* include cash in the vault and deposits at the central bank.
7 SDRs are IMF-issued checking accounts that provide additional international liquidity to central bank or government members. The SDR's value is a weighted average of five currencies, namely, the British pound, Chinese yuan, Euro Area euro, Japanese yen, and U.S. dollar.
8 As is the case with FA, readers (especially those familiar with BPM5) should beware of the signs attached to RRI transactions because they are the opposite of BPM5.
9 In *Chapter 10: Central bank tools and monetary policy*, we will find that a nation's monetary base decreases when the central bank reduces its official reserves and increases when it acquires them.

7 An overview of financial markets

Healthy economies have stable, growing, and developing financial markets. This chapter introduces financial markets and discusses some important terms used to describe them.

Debt versus equity markets

Financial markets can be separated into two major parts, debt and equity. Debt markets are where interest-earning financial instruments are bought and sold. The interest rates on these instruments may be fixed until maturity or variable, in which case they depend on evolving market conditions. Borrowers have legal obligations to service these liabilities by promptly making periodic interest and amortization payments, as well as paying any remaining principal, at maturity. The owners of debt instruments are different from stockholders, because they have no voting power in the issuing companies and have no upward potential if the borrowers' profits rise.

Equity markets, which are often called stock markets, are where partial ownership claims on companies are bought and sold. Stockholders have voting rights in the issuing companies, but they have no legal right to receive dividends or any return on their initial investments. Rather, shareholders are residual claimants on a company's cash flows, profits, and assets, which means, after everyone else is paid, the rest goes to shareholders in the form of dividends and stock appreciation, or if the company fails, they receive net liquidation proceeds. Stocks are usually considered to be more risky than debt instruments because their returns have higher volatilities, and their owners are residual claimants, rather than creditors who must be paid, by borrowers, to avoid default.

Money versus capital markets

Financial markets are often described by the maturity of the instruments issued and traded. Money markets are where financial assets with maturities less than or equal to one year are bought and sold. Capital markets are where interest-earning assets with maturities greater than one year, as well as stocks, are bought and sold.[1] Examples of money market instruments are checking accounts, currency (i.e., paper bills and coins), 90-day government Treasury bills, commercial paper,[2] and certificates of deposit. Capital market instruments include corporate and government bonds and notes, as well as stocks. Therefore, 20-year residential and commercial mortgages, 10-year government bonds, 5-year corporate notes, and shares in companies, such as Alibaba, Cemex, Microsoft, Royal Dutch Shell, and Toyota, are all part of the capital market.

Primary versus secondary markets

Financial instruments are first offered for sale on primary markets, which means they are the true sources of funds for companies, governments, and individuals that borrow. Once issued, the financial assets of well-recognized borrowers can be purchased and sold freely on secondary markets, but these financial transactions are not net sources of *new* funds for a nation's financial system.

Helpful information about debt and equity yields, returns, and prices

Understanding a few basic facts about debt and equity instruments can help reduce confusion about how international macroeconomics treats and analyzes financial markets.

Inverse relationship between debt prices and interest yields

There is an inverse relationship between a debt instrument's price and interest yield. A simple example explains why. Suppose a government bill promises to repay $100 in one year, and it is auctioned today at a price of $90. To the investor, the return on this security (also called its yield or interest rate) would be 11.1 percent (see Figure 7.1). To the borrower, 11.1 percent would be the cost of credit. By contrast, if the auction price was $80, the interest rate would rise to 25 percent, and at a price of $75, this yield would increase to 33.3 percent. Therefore, the lower a debt instrument's price, the higher its yield; or, conversely, higher yields imply lower debt instrument prices.

Now	**Next Year**	
Debt Instrument's Price	**Repayment Amount**	**Interest Yield (Also Called Cost of Credit)**
$90	$100	$\dfrac{\$10}{\$90} \times 100\% = 11.1\%$
$80	$100	$\dfrac{\$20}{\$80} \times 100\% = 25.0\%$
$75	$100	$\dfrac{\$25}{\$75} \times 100 = 33.3\%$

Figure 7.1 Relationship between a debt instrument's price and interest yield.

What determines stock prices, and why do they change?

Stock prices are reported daily in the business news and actively followed by a broad spectrum of interested onlookers – from institutional investors to politicians to most of us trying to build our wealth, save for retirement, and prepare for rainy days. A stock's price is determined by two major factors, namely fundamentals and animal spirits. Due to animal spirits, which are prompted by changes in expectations, stock prices can vary substantially from their fundamental valuations. Yet, it is important (and a bit reassuring) to note that these prices eventually return to their fundamental values.

What determines a stock's fundamental value?

The fundamental value of a stock depends on three major factors: (1) expectations of future profits, (2) risks, and (3) the returns on alternative investments.

EXPECTATION OF FUTURE PROFITS

Stockholders are the residual claimants of a company's cash flows, profits, and assets. Therefore, if a company's expected stream of future earnings increases, stockholders can anticipate being the beneficiaries, which means the fundamental value of their shares should increase.

RISKS

Greater risks reduce equity prices. Given two financial assets, A and B, with the same expected return, if financial Asset A is riskless and financial Asset B is not, investors will demand the safer asset, causing the risky one's price to fall.

RETURNS ON ALTERNATIVE INVESTMENTS

The return on alternative investment assets has an inverse relationship with a stock's price. For instance, if the return on interest-earning debt instruments rises relative to the expected return on stocks, investors will increase their demands for debt instruments and decrease their demands for equities, causing stock prices to fall. In fact, investors are likely to sell stocks to free cash, which can then be used to purchase the higher-yielding debt instruments. As a rule of thumb, because equities involve default risks (also called credit risks), they should earn at least as much as a risk-free debt instrument, such as the return on a security issued by a credible (i.e., financially healthy and trustworthy) government.

Animal spirits

"Animal spirits" is a term coined by John Maynard Keynes, a famous 20th-century economist, to explain changes in the supply and demand for stocks that are based on investor and borrower instincts, preferences, biases, emotions, egos, and exuberance – not fundamentals. These animal spirits can cause stock prices to vary considerably from their fundamentals and are the basis for many speculators' financial successes or failures.

Inverse relationship between stock prices and interest yields

From our discussion of returns on alternative investments (above), one point is clear. As interest yields on debt securities rise, the prices of stocks fall (and vice versa), which means both stock and debt prices bear inverse relationships to interest yields. This fact will be important for the remainder of this book and is re-emphasized in the next section.

International macroeconomics combines debt and equity markets

International macroeconomics is most interested in the average cost and quantity of *all* funds borrowed and lent per period – regardless of their sources or uses. Therefore, it streamlines its analyses by aggregating the markets for loans, interest-bearing money market and capital market debt instruments, and stocks. The combined sources and uses of borrowed and lent funds per period are referred to as *credit*, and its average price is called the *cost of credit (*or *yield* or *interest rate).*[3] Therefore, *cost of credit, interest*, and *yield* are proxies for average borrowing and lending rates on interest-earning securities and average expected stock returns. This simplification makes sense because the price of money market, capital market, and stock market securities all bear the same inverse relationship to the cost of credit. If the cost of credit falls, the prices of these financial securities rise, and if it rises, they fall. In short, because the prices of all these investment assets move in the same direction when credit supply or demand change, there is no need to distinguish between the different financial market segments.

Portfolio composition

Investors change the composition of their portfolios based on movements in relative market signals, such as risk-adjusted returns among investment assets, availability of liquidity, and expectations. We will find in *Chapter 10: Central bank tools and monetary policy* that these portfolio adjustments provide a major channel through which monetary policy affects economic activity.

Conclusion

Financial markets have multiple sources and uses of funds, such as loans, interest-earning securities, and stocks. Economists aggregate and refer to them, simply, as the CR market, in which the cost of credit and amount of credit supplied and demanded per period are determined.

Notes

1 Derivative markets are ignored here because they are not ultimate sources of funding.
2 Well-known companies often issue commercial paper (i.e., a short-term, unsecured promissory note) directly to borrowers when they want to finance their working capital (i.e., day-to-day operating) needs.
3 When the expected inflation component is removed, it is called the *real* cost of credit (or *real* interest rate).

8 Credit market

The credit (CR) market is the third and final sector in our macroeconomic trinity.[1] This chapter explains the important difference between the real and nominal cost of credit, how real credit costs are determined, and why they change. As is the case with all market prices, the fundamental causes of equilibrium rates and changes in them are the forces of supply and demand.

Nominal versus real credit costs

The cost of credit comes in two major forms, nominal and real. The *nominal cost of credit* is what we read about and hear reported on the evening news. It is the interest we pay when we borrow and the rates we earn when we lend, invest, and deposit funds. The nominal cost of credit is composed of the *real cost of credit* and *inflationary expectations* (see Figure 8.1). The *real cost of*

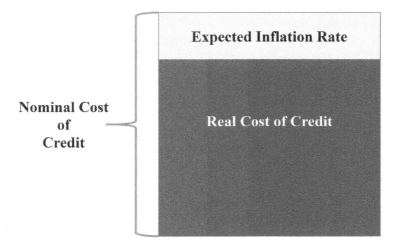

Figure 8.1 Major components of the nominal cost of credit.

credit is what we expect to pay or earn after the effects of anticipated inflation have stripped away purchasing power. Rational individuals and businesses should make decisions based on real credit costs – not nominal costs. The next section explains why.

Expected inflation premium and expected deflation discount

The real cost of credit is the percent by which lenders' actual purchasing power increases and borrowers' purchasing power decreases when a debt is repaid. Inflation reduces the purchasing power of money, and deflation increases it. Therefore, if a lender expects to earn (and a borrower expects to pay) a 2 percent real credit cost, then the nominal cost should equal 2 percent only if expected inflation equals 0 percent. By contrast, if the real cost of credit is 2 percent and expected inflation is 3 percent, lenders should charge and borrowers should be willing to pay 5 percent. By agreeing to a 5 percent rate and having inflation erode 3 percent of its value, credit suppliers end with 2 percent more purchasing power, and borrowers end with 2 percent less.

What happens when reality does not match expectations? For example, consider what would happen if lenders and borrowers expected inflation to be 3 percent and charged a 5 percent nominal interest rate, but during the year prices increased by 4 percent. At 4 percent, inflation would reduce the lenders' real return to 1 percent (i.e., the 5 percent nominal cost of credit minus the 4 percent inflation rate) and reduce the burden on the borrowers. By contrast, if inflation turned out to be lower than 3 percent (say, 1 percent), then the outcome would be the opposite. Lower-than-expected inflation would help lenders by providing them with higher-than-expected real returns and harm borrowers, who would repay more (in real terms) than they expected. Therefore, lenders are hurt and borrowers helped when actual inflation is greater than expected, and lenders are helped and borrowers are hurt when the opposite occurs.

Because unexpected inflation can have unwanted redistributive effects, some central banks, such as the U.S. Fed, Bank of England, and Bank of Japan, have used *forward guidance*[2] techniques to signal their future monetary policy intentions or announced goals, such as inflation targets. For these policy tools to have stabilizing influences, the central bank using them needs to have earned credibility and public trust.

There are two major take-aways from this section:

- First, as expected inflation rises, the nominal cost of credit should increase, and expected deflation should have just the opposite effect.
- Second, if the actual inflation rate ends up equaling expected inflation and the nominal cost of credit incorporates this expectation, then

inflation should have no financial-market redistribution effects, because borrowers and lenders are neither harmed nor helped by it.

Determining a nation's real cost of credit and quantity of real credit per period

The cost and quantity per period of real (i.e., inflation-adjusted) credit is determined by the forces of supply and demand. Let's investigate more carefully the factors that influence real credit demand and supply, as well as the variables that cause these forces to change.

Effects of real credit costs on the amount of credit demanded and supplied per period

Credit is demanded when households, businesses, governments, and foreign residents borrow. One of the primary factors influencing the amount borrowed is the real cost of credit. A rising cost discourages borrowing by making credit more expensive, and a lower cost encourages borrowing. See Figure 8.2.

Funds are supplied to the CR markets by domestic and foreign households, businesses, governments, and central banks. Households supply funds when they save. Businesses supply them via retained earnings that are invested in

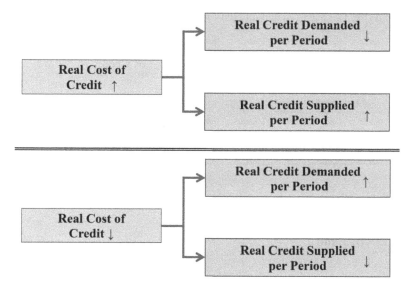

Figure 8.2 Effect of real credit costs on the quantity of real credit demanded and supplied per period.

nonoperating assets, such as bonds. State, local, and national governments supply funds when they run budget surpluses and invest them in interest-earning securities or repurchase outstanding bonds. Foreigners supply credit when they invest financially in international CR markets, and central banks supply funds when they create new money. Central banks are particularly important suppliers of funds, which is why *Chapter 10: Central bank tools and monetary policy* discusses how monetary authorities change the supply of credit and the rationale behind their policies. Figure 8.2 shows that an increase in the real cost of credit encourages households, businesses, governments, and foreigners to supply more funds to the market, and a lower interest rate discourages it.

Effects when external factors change real credit demand and supply

The real cost of credit is not the only economic factor that influences the supply of and demand for credit. Movements in other external factors can have significant effects on demand and/or supply.

What happens to real credit cost and quantity per period when demand and supply change?

Consequences of changing real credit demand

As the demand for real credit rises, its cost and the quantity of real credit per period rise. Decreases in demand have just the opposite effects. See Figure 8.3.

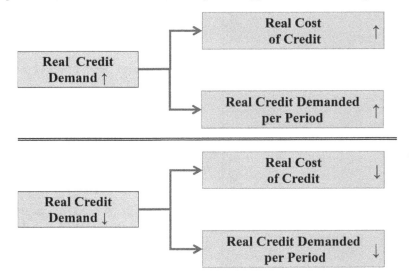

Figure 8.3 Effects of changing real credit demand.

Consequences of changing real credit supply

Increases in the supply of real credit by savers, lenders, and investors reduce real credit costs and increase the quantity of real credit per period. Reductions in supply have exactly the opposite effect, causing the real cost of credit to rise and quantity of real credit per period to fall. See Figure 8.4.

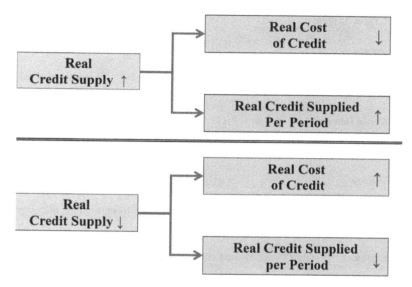

Figure 8.4 Effects of changing real credit supply.

Consequences of changing real credit demand *and* supply

What happens to the cost and quantity of real credit per period when demand *and* supply change simultaneously?

Consequences if real credit demand and supply change in the same direction

When real credit demand and supply move in the same direction, the qualitative movement in the quantity per period is certain, but the change in real credit cost is uncertain (see Figure 8.5). Therefore, if real credit demand and supply increase simultaneously, the quantity of funds traded in the CR market per period must rise, but the change in real credit cost is uncertain. If demand and supply decrease simultaneously, the quantity of real credit per period must fall, but the change in real credit cost is, again, uncertain.

Cause		Effects	
	Movement	Real Cost of Credit	Quantity of Real Credit per Period
Real Credit Demand	↑	↑	↑
Real Credit Supply	↑	↓	↑
Net Change		Uncertain	↑
	Movement	Real Cost of Credit	Quantity of Real Credit per Period
Real Credit Demand	↓	↓	↓
Real Credit Supply	↓	↑	↓
Net Change		Uncertain	↓

Figure 8.5 Effects when real credit demand and supply shift in the same direction.

Consequences if credit demand and supply change in opposite directions

Figure 8.6 shows the results when the real credit supply and demand change in opposite directions. An increase in demand causes both the cost and quantity of real credit per period to rise. A decrease in supply causes the real cost of credit to rise but the quantity per period to fall. Therefore, when the demand for real credit rises and supply falls, the real cost of credit must rise, but the change in quantity is uncertain (see Figure 8.6 – top panel). Conversely, a decrease in real credit demand and increase in supply cause the real cost of credit to fall and the change in quantity per period to be uncertain (see Figure 8.6 – bottom panel).

External factors that influence the cost of credit

Let's step back for a moment to consider some of the important external factors that influence the demand for and supply of real (inflation-adjusted) credit per period. Some of them influence only demand, others affect only supply, and still others affect both demand and supply, simultaneously.

Cause	Effects		
	Movement	**Real Cost of Credit**	**Real Credit per Period**
Real Credit Demand	↑	↑	↑
Real Credit Supply	↓	↑	↓
Net Change		↑	**Uncertain**
	Movement	**Real Cost of Credit**	**Real Credit per Period**
Real Credit Demand	↓	↓	↓
Real Credit Supply	↑	↓	↑
Net Change		↓	**Uncertain**

Figure 8.6 Effects when real credit demand and supply shift in opposite directions.

External factors that affect real credit demand

Business investments

When businesses are unable to internally fund investment opportunities that arise, they turn to the CR market. Increases in I raise credit demand, thereby, causing the cost and quantity of real credit per period to rise. Reductions in I have the opposite effect.

Consumer demand for housing and nondurable goods

Real credit demand is also affected by consumers, mainly those wishing to purchase homes and durable goods, such as automobiles, home appliances, and furniture. When such purchases cannot be funded from monthly paychecks or savings, households turn to the credit markets. Greater consumer purchases of these products increase the demand for credit, causing the cost and quantity of real credit per period to rise. Reductions have the opposite effect.

Government budget deficits

Rising government deficits increase the demand for credit, thereby, raising the cost and quantity of real credit per period. Falling budget deficits have the opposite effects.

International financial capital outflows

Financial capital outflows from Nation A occur when foreign residents increase their demands for funds in Nation A's CR market. They also occur when foreign returns are relatively higher than in Nation A, causing individuals and businesses to borrow Nation A's currency, convert it to foreign currencies, and then invest in the foreign assets. These borrowers increase the demand for real credit in Nation A, which raises its cost and quantity per period. Reductions in these outflows decrease the demand for real credit in Nation A, causing its cost and quantity per period to fall.

External factors that change real credit supply

Government budget surpluses

Rising government surpluses increase the supply of real credit, thereby, reducing its cost and increasing the quantity per period. Falling surpluses have the opposite effects.

Saving[3]

When households save greater portions of their incomes, the supply of real credit rises, causing its cost to fall and quantity per period to rise. Reductions in saving have the opposite effects.

International financial capital inflows

International capital inflows occur when foreign residents invest funds in Nation A or lend funds to Nation A's residents. Increased inflows raise the supply of real credit in Nation A, causing its cost to fall and quantity per period to rise. Reductions in these financial capital inflows have the opposite effects.

Household wealth

Increases in household wealth reduce families' need to save for retirement and precautionary purposes, causing a reduction in real credit supply, which increases its cost and reduces the quantity per period.

Central bank money creation

The creation of money by a central bank increases the supply of real credit, which lowers its cost and increases the quantity per period.[4] Reductions in the real money supply have the opposite effects.

Risks

Lenders expect to be compensated for the risks they take in extending credit. When these risks fall, lenders supply more funds to the real credit market, thereby reducing its cost and increasing the quantity per period. The risks that enter most prominently into the real cost of credit are (1) market risks; (2) political, monetary, economic, and social risks; and (3) default risks.

Market risks are due to unexpected changes in economic variables that influence the net cash flows (e.g., profitability) of borrowers. The more volatile these variables, the higher the risk premium that is incorporated into the real cost of credit.

Political, monetary, economic, and social risks reflect the stability, integrity, and fairness of existing and expected governments, central banks, economic systems, and social structures. The higher these risks, the greater the expected real return must be, which means the lower the supply of real credit.

Default (credit) risk reflects the chances that a borrower will be unable or unwilling to pay its credit obligations, usually due to insolvency and/or illiquidity. Insolvency occurs when the value of a borrower's liabilities exceeds its assets, and illiquidity occurs when a borrower has insufficient funds to meet maturing obligations. This difference is important because many solvent companies have failed due their inability to fund daily operations.

Many financial risks are diversifiable, which means, if lenders and investors purchase a broad range of financial assets, they can expect to earn less-than-average returns on some of their risky assets and more-than-average returns on others, thereby bringing their overall returns to stable levels. Therefore, risks that are not diversifiable pose the greatest threats to lenders and investors.

External factors that simultaneously change real credit demand and supply

RGDP

If RGDP rises, household incomes and business profits increase, causing saving to grow and, with it, the supply of real credit. Increases in RGDP also strengthen the demand for credit, as businesses borrow to finance capacity expansions and larger inventories. Finally, higher RGDP increases government tax revenues and lowers the unemployment rate, which reduces government transfers for social welfare programs. Therefore, the combined effect of rising tax revenues and falling transfers reduces budget deficits and the government's demand for credit. Because the overall change in demand is uncertain and the supply of real credit rises, no conclusion can be drawn about net changes in the cost or quantity per period of real credit when RGDP rises.

Falling RGDP reduces saving, which decreases the supply of real credit. It also reduces company investments, which decreases businesses' demand for real credit. Finally, lower RGDP reduces tax revenues and increases social welfare transfers, which increase government deficits and its demand for real credit. Therefore, due to the conflicting supply and demand forces, no conclusion can be drawn about changes in the cost or quantity per period of real credit when RGDP falls.

Household income tax rates

Higher income tax rates reduce households' after-tax incomes, which lowers their ability to save and, therefore, reduces the supply of real credit. At the same time, these tax revenues flow to the government, thereby reducing its budget deficits and the demand for real credit. While the reduction in real credit supply and demand *seem* to cause an uncertain change in the real cost of credit, under normal conditions the demand-side effects should outweigh the supply-side ones. We know this because a dollar of increased tax revenues reduces the government's budget deficit by a full dollar, but the same tax dollar reduces household saving by only a portion of that dollar. As households' after-tax income falls, they also decrease consumption.

Household and business indebtedness levels

Increased household and business indebtedness levels reduce their ability to borrow, causing the demand for credit per period to fall. In addition, as these indebtedness levels rise, households and businesses are forced to economize and repay their debts, causing the supply of real credit to rise. Overall, the decrease in real credit demand and increase in supply cause the cost of real credit to fall and the change in quantity per period to be uncertain. Falling household and business indebtedness levels have the opposite effects.

Expectations and regulations

Changes in expectations and regulations can have considerable effects on the cost of credit. Often, the change in supply and demand reinforce each other, causing predictable changes in the cost of credit, such as when a nation is at war, rule of law is violated by a government, or central bank policies lack credibility.

Examples

Let's use a few examples to internalize the cause-and-effect relationships between movements in external economic factors and changes in a nation's *real* cost of credit, *nominal* cost of credit, and quantity of real credit per period.

Money creation by the U.S. Federal Reserve

Suppose the Federal Reserve increased U.S. money supply. The increased supply of credit would reduce the real cost of credit and increase the real credit quantity per period (see Figure 8.4 – top panel).

As for the nominal cost of credit, greater borrowing and spending are likely to increase expected inflation, which could partially or fully offset the reduction in real credit cost. Therefore, the nominal cost of credit could rise, fall, or remain the same. This uncertainty is relatively less important, because movements in real credit costs should influence rational borrowing and lending decisions more than nominal yields.

Increased British government spending financed by borrowing

Suppose the English government increased spending and financed it by borrowing funds in the pound CR market. The increased demand for funds would raise England's real credit cost and quantity of real credit per period (see Figure 8.3 – top panel). As for the nominal cost of credit, greater borrowing and spending are likely to increase expected inflation, which would reinforce the increase in real credit cost and cause the nominal cost of credit to rise.

Foreign instability causing a flight to safety

Suppose investors were frightened by turbulent economic, political, and social unrest in the Middle East and decided to invest financially in less-risky Swiss financial assets. This *flight to safety* would increase the supply of funds to Switzerland, thereby reducing Switzerland's real credit costs and increasing the quantity of real Swiss franc credit per period (see Figure 8.4 – top panel).

Conclusion

Even though most of us are more familiar with the nominal cost of credit than its real cost, rational borrowers and lenders should be influenced more by real than nominal credit rates. The real cost of credit is determined in open financial markets by the forces of supply and demand. By identifying the factors that cause such changes, one can better explain the direction in which interest rates are moving, have moved, and will move.

Notes

1 The other markets are the G&S market and FX market.
2 Forward guidance will be discussed, again, in *Chapter 10: Central bank tools and monetary policy.*
3 Economists distinguish between saving and saving*s*. Saving (i.e., no "s" at the end) measures what is left each period after we subtract consumption and taxes from our incomes. Saving is always measured over periods of time. By contrast, saving*s* (notice the "s" at the end) is the net accumulation of all the saving people have done. Therefore, it is always measured at a point in time.
4 This relationship will be clarified in *Chapter 9: Money, banking, and central banks* and *Chapter 10: Central bank tools and monetary policy.*

9   Money, banking, and central banks

This chapter defines the monetary aggregates that are commonly used by central banks to measure liquidity levels in their financial systems. It goes on to explain how money is created by financial institutions, such as banks, and the role a nation's monetary base and money multiplier play in creating money.

What is money?

The assets included in a nation's money supply are part of the *money market* because they have maturities less than or equal to one year. Many people are surprised to learn that most nations have more than one money supply measure. Central banks use the one that has proven to have the closest correlation to their goals, such as low and steady inflation, full employment, and/or targeted exchange rate levels. Money supply definitions are organic in the sense they change when novel financial instruments are introduced and substantially affect spending and financial investment patterns or decisions.[1]

M1

The narrowest money supply measure is M1, which includes currency in circulation (i.e., paper bills and coins *outside banks*) plus checking accounts (see Figure 9.1). Credit cards are not included until they are used. Similarly, the currency in bank vaults is not counted because it does not affect potential purchasing power until these funds are outside the bank and in the hands of businesses and individuals, who can spend them.

M2 and M3

M2 is composed of everything in M1 plus *near money*, which includes other short-term financial assets, that a central bank determines have significant

M1	≡	Currency in Circulation + Checking Accounts
M2	≡	M1 + Very Liquid *Near-Money* Financial Assets
M3	≡	M2 + Less Liquid *Near-Money* Financial Assets

Figure 9.1 Money supply measures.

impacts on spending, such as savings accounts and money market mutual funds held by individuals (see Figure 9.1). M3 includes everything in M2 plus other, near-money financial assets that are either slightly less liquid than those in M2, such as large time deposits, or M2-like assets that are unlikely to be spent, such as money market mutual funds held by institutional investors (see Figure 9.1).

Central bank mandate(s)

A central bank's main responsibility is keeping inflation under control. Therefore, if a nation's inflation rate is persistently higher and less stable than desired, it is usually the central bank that is held accountable. Some nations have broadened their central banks' mandates to include low unemployment rates, fixed exchange rates, and/or financial stability.

Many countries and currency unions insulate their central banks from government intervention and political pressures by legislating their independence. If history has taught us anything, it is elevated and less stable inflation rates have a greater likelihood of occurring when central banks (the ultimate money creators) are tied too closely to national governments (the ultimate spenders).

How do central banks control their nations' money supplies?

Before explaining the tools central banks use to control their money supply levels, it is worthwhile gaining perspective into the general relationship between a central bank and the rest of the economy. This is done in the next section by using the *above-the-line/below-the-line* concept.

Above the line/below the line

To visualize the role a central bank plays in an economy, imagine a horizontal line drawn across a page, such as the one in Figure 9.2. Imagine further a nation's central bank above the line, and all other economic participants,

Central Bank

Above the Line

Below the Line

Only money below the line influences G&S demand.

Financial Institutions   **Businesses**   **Households**   **Governments**

Figure 9.2 Above the line/below the line.

such as domestic and foreign financial institutions (e.g., banks), businesses, households, and governments, below it.

This horizontal line is important because only the funds below it are part of a nation's money supply and affect G&S demand. The central bank's job is to supply participants below the line with enough liquidity (i.e., money) to effectively and efficiently carry out their daily activities. Too much liquidity could create unwanted inflation, and too little could cause deflation and recession. A central bank influences liquidity levels by changing the ability of financial institutions (below the line) to lend, and it accomplishes this goal by increasing or decreasing the nation's or currency area's *monetary base* and/or *money multiplier*. Let's discuss these two important macroeconomic concepts.

Monetary base

Monetary base is the raw material from which a banking system creates money. It includes currency in circulation and bank reserves, which are composed of cash that banks hold in their vaults and their deposits at the central bank.

Why would a bank deposit funds at the central bank? One reason is for check-clearing purposes; another is to earn a safe rate of return, but equally important is central banks require financial institutions to hold reserves in proportion to their customers' deposits. For example, if the reserve requirement ratio is 10 percent, then banks must keep $10 in reserves for every $100 a customer deposits. Most of these reserves are held on deposit at the central bank and not as cash in the vault.

In any economic discussion about money, it is important to remember that only a central bank can create monetary base. It does so by crossing our imaginary horizontal line and purchasing assets from individuals and businesses or by lending funds to financial institutions, like banks (see Figure 9.3). In both cases, the central bank simply writes checks on itself to pay for these assets or to fund the loans, which means the potential for excessive monetary base creation is significant. This potential is especially true for nations that have no precious metal(s) (e.g., gold or silver) backing their currencies, which is the case for most nations in the world.[2]

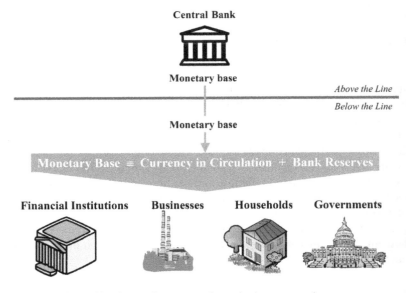

Figure 9.3 Central banks are the source of a nation's monetary base.

When monetary base is injected below the line by a central bank, a large portion (or all) of these funds end up in banks, and profit-minded bankers lend them or use the funds to purchase financial assets. As the banking system lends and relends these funds, the nation's money supply grows larger than the initial injection of monetary base. This amplification effect is called the *money multiplier*, which is the topic of the next section.

Money multiplier

An example might help to explain the money multiplier concept (see Figure 9.4).

- Suppose the U.S. Federal Reserve injects $100 million of newly created monetary base into the U.S. economy by purchasing government bonds from individuals and companies who need funds to purchase residential homes and commercial real estate. The sellers of these securities would deposit the newly created funds into their bank checking accounts. At this point, the U.S. money supply would increase by $100 million, because M1 includes checking accounts, which have just increased by $100 million.[3]
- Notice in Figure 9.4 that the first bank (Bank A) receives $100 million but lends only $80 million. The full $100 million is not lent because banks must keep a portion of their customer deposits to meet central bank reserve requirements. If this requirement is 10 percent, then Bank A would need to hold reserve assets equaling $10 million. In addition, Bank A would have incentives to retain a portion of these funds for other reasons. Let's assume that it holds an additional $3 million to meet potential customer withdrawals and $7 million for precautionary reasons. Therefore, of the original $100 million, Bank A holds

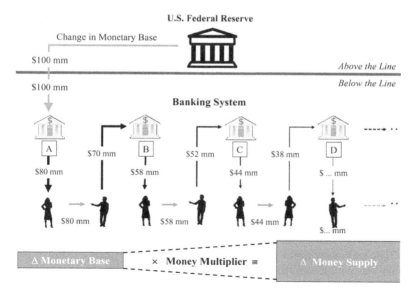

Figure 9.4 Money multiplier.

$20 million (i.e., $10 million + $3 million + $7 million = $20 million) and lends the rest ($80 million).
- Bank A lends the $80 million by increasing the checking accounts of borrowers, which raises the nation's money supply (e.g., M1) by this amount.[4]
- After the loan is spent, the first borrower loses her $80 million checking account, but the recipient gains it. Therefore, M1 remains $80 million higher, because one checking account falls by the same amount another rises.
- At this point, the recipient has the choice of keeping all or a portion of these funds in the bank. Suppose he keeps $70 million in his checking account and withdraws the rest ($10 million) in cash.
- The bank receiving this $70 million checking deposit (Bank B) needs to hold 10 percent (i.e., $7 million) as required reserves. In addition, suppose it holds an additional $5 million to meet potential customer withdrawals and for precautionary purposes. The remaining portion of the original $70 million deposit equals $58 million, which can be lent to a new borrower by increasing her checking account by this amount. As a result, the nation's money supply increases by an additional $58 million. See Figure 9.4.
- Of the $58 million lent, suppose $52 million is deposited back into Bank C, thereby giving another bank new funds to lend. Of this amount, assume Bank C lends $44 million.
- On and on this process would go, in recurring *lend-spend-redeposit* cycles, until there is nothing left to lend.

Let's step back from this example to understand the consequences of the central bank's initial injection of monetary base and the subsequent lend-spend-redeposit cycle. In our example, the Fed injects $100 million into the U.S. financial system, and the initial infusion causes the M1 money supply to rise by $100 million. Afterwards, the lend-spend-redeposit cycle causes checking accounts to rise by $80 million, $58 million, $44 million, and so on until the lending power of the banking system is exhausted. If we add up just the first four rounds, it is clear that the U.S. money supply has already increased by a multiple of the initial injection of monetary base. In fact, activity in the first four rounds increases M1 by $282 million (i.e., $100 million + $80 million + $58 million + $44 million = $282 million), and there is still lending potential in the banking system.

The take-away point is any time a central bank increases a nation's monetary base, it creates the potential for an amplified increase in the nation's money supply. Therefore, by controlling banks' ability to lend, a central bank can influence the nation's money supply.

Who else influences the money multiplier?

Central banks do not have exclusive control over the money multiplier. In general, any time the actions of households, businesses, or financial institutions change the lending potential of the banking system, the money multiplier changes. For example, if individuals deposit relatively more cash in banks, rather than keep it as currency in circulation, or if the banks are willing to lend greater portions of their excess reserves (e.g., rather than keep them for precautionary reasons), the banking system's lending ability rises – and, therefore, so does the money multiplier. Similarly, because the reserve requirement on near money deposits is usually lower than on checking accounts, any shift in customer preferences toward near money deposits and away from checking accounts increases the money multiplier.

Conclusion

A primary measure of a nation's liquidity is its money supply, which is tracked, reported, and managed by central banks. The focus of a central bank's attention is the money supply measure that, it believes, has the greatest effect on important macroeconomic variables, such as prices, RGDP, and exchange rates. Because the closeness of this relationship varies from nation to nation, some central banks focus on M1, while other focus on M2 or M3. Central banks control the liquidity in a nation or currency area by changing the monetary base and/or money multiplier.

Notes

1 For this reason, virtual currencies, such as bitcoin, ether, and/or central-bank-created virtual currencies, may one day change the official way nations define money.
2 When a country chooses to back its currency with a precious metal, the central bank loses much of its ability to independently influence the money supply, which could be good or bad, depending on the competence and credibility of the central bank. What is often ignored is that commodity-backed currency systems, such as the gold standard, create a host of other problems.
3 To simplify the explanation, Figure 9.4 shows just one bank receiving the entire $100 million, but the results would be identical if many banks received the funds.
4 To simplify the explanation, Figure 9.4 shows just one individual borrowing the entire $80 million, but the results would be identical with many borrowers.

10   Central bank tools and monetary policy

Central banks and other financial regulators have three major responsibilities, namely to (1) control their nations' or currency areas' liquidity levels by changing the money supply, (2) supervise individual financial institutions to ensure their health and soundness, and (3) protect against systemic risks that could threaten their entire financial systems. Regulating liquidity levels is done via *monetary policies*, supervising individual financial institutions is the focus of *microprudential* regulations, and controlling the negative externalities of systemic risks is the domain of *macroprudential* regulations.

Central bank monetary tools

Central banks have five major monetary tools to change their nations' or currency areas' money supplies. These tools are: (1) open market operations, (2) FX market intervention, (3) the discount rate, (4) the percent of customers' deposits that must be held by banks as required reserves, and (5) the nominal interest rate that banks receive on the reserves they deposit at the central bank. A distinguishing characteristic that separates these tools is whether they affect the monetary base or money multiplier.

Central bank tools that affect the monetary base

Three of the five monetary tools affect a nation's monetary base, namely, (1) open market operations, (2) FX market intervention, and/or (3) discount rate.

Open market operations

Open market operations are purchases and sales of financial assets that a central bank transacts with individuals and businesses below the line. This tool's name is descriptive because securities (usually government securities) are normally bought and sold in open markets and not directly from governments or their original issuers.

To understand the effect open market operations have on a nation's monetary base and money supply, let's use an example. Suppose the U.S. Federal Reserve purchased $100 million of U.S. government securities from individuals and businesses (below the line). Payment of $100 million would be made to the owners of these securities, and they would deposit the newly created funds in checking accounts at their banks. The banking system would be required to hold a portion of these deposits as required reserves but could lend the rest. As Figure 10.1 shows, these funds would enter the lend-spend-redeposit cycle and increase the nation's money supply by a multiplier effect.

FX market intervention

FX market intervention involves purchases and sales of foreign currencies that central banks transact with counterparties below the line. Figure 10.1 shows that, if Federal Reserve purchased $100 million worth of euros from individuals below the line, the U.S. monetary base and money supply would rise by the same amount as with open market operations. In the FX market, $100 million would be paid to the owners of the euros, who would deposit the newly created dollars in their checking accounts, leaving the U.S. financial system with $100 million in new monetary base and banks with excess reserves to lend.[1] These funds would enter the lend-spend-redeposit cycle and expand the nation's money supply by a multiplier effect.

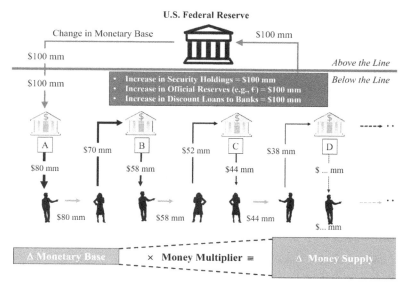

Figure 10.1 Central bank actions that affect the monetary base.

Discount rate

The *discount rate* is the nominal interest rate that a central bank charges on loans it makes to financial intermediaries (below the line). By increasing this rate, central banks discourage bank borrowing, and by lowering it, they encourage borrowing. In Figure 10.1, discount loans directly increase bank reserves by $100 million, leaving the banking system with funds to lend and relend. As before, these funds enter the lend-spend-redeposit cycle and expand the nation's money supply by a multiplier effect.

New monetary tools used by central banks to change the monetary base

In general, whenever a central bank purchases or sells any asset (financial or real) that resides below the line, the nation's or currency area's monetary base changes. It makes no difference whether the asset was (1) issued by a government or private company; (2) purchased in the secondary (i.e., already issued) or primary (i.e., newly issued) markets; or (3) an interest-earning security, such as a bill, note, or bond, an equity share (i.e., stock), or a physical asset (e.g., truck, plane, or snowblower). Central banks prefer to purchase safe, short-term government securities, such as Treasury bills, that are issued in the domestic currency because these assets minimize both credit (i.e., default) and market risks.

Despite their preference for safe, short-term financial assets, extenuating circumstances have pushed central banks to purchase and sell progressively riskier assets. For years, some central banks, such as the Swiss National Bank, have purchased and sold currencies in the broad and deep FX markets – especially when they wished to diversify their reserve assets and/or when the domestic government debt markets were relatively thin. During and after the Great Recession (2007 to 2009), when short-term nominal interest rates were pushed to zero (and sometimes below zero), central banks, such as the Bank of Japan, Bank of England, European Central Bank, and U.S. Federal Reserve, diversified into other financial assets, such as long-term government bonds and regional government bonds. Soon thereafter, they branched into corporate bonds, exchange-traded funds, shares of individual private companies (e.g., Apple and Coca-Cola), and financial real estate instruments.

Central bank tools that affect the money multiplier

Of the five monetary tools, two affect a nation's money multiplier. They are the (1) required reserve ratio and (2) nominal interest rate banks earn on the reserves they deposit at the central bank.

Required reserve ratio

The required reserve ratio is the percent of reserve assets (i.e., cash in banks' vaults and deposits at the central bank) that banks are required to hold against customers' deposits. In the previous section, banks were required to hold 10 percent of every dollar deposited with them, and they voluntarily held more for customer withdrawal and precautionary reasons. Therefore, they could lend a maximum of 90 cents on each dollar deposited, if they held only required reserves. If the central bank lowered this reserve requirement to 5 percent, then the banks' ability to lend (and create money) would increase, because they would now have the potential to lend more (e.g., 95 percent instead of 90 percent) of each dollar deposited. A lower reserve requirement ratio empowers banks to lend more, and a higher requirement disempowers them.

Nominal interest rate on bank deposits at the central bank

Some (but not all) central banks pay interest on bank deposits, which leaves these financial intermediaries with an important choice regarding what to do with their excess reserves. If the funds are lent to customers, they may earn higher rates of return, but these borrowers could also default, which would significantly reduce banks' earnings. If the funds are deposited at the central bank, principal repayment and regular interest earnings would be assured, but banks would earn lower rates of return. By raising the central bank deposit rate, banks are discouraged from lending to customers, causing the money multiplier to fall. By contrast, reducing this interest rate encourages loans to customers, which increases the money multiplier.

Notice in Figure 10.2 how the rectangle on the lower left side, which represents the monetary base, has not changed in size, but the money supply rectangle on the lower right side, which represents the change in money supply, has increased due to the lower required reserve ratio or lower deposit rate at the central bank, both of which increase the money multiplier.

Monetary policy

G&S demand equals $C + I + G + NE$. Therefore, a central bank can influence this demand only if it is able to change one (or more) of these components without incurring offsetting adjustments in others. A central bank can influence G&S demand through multiple channels. Three of the most important are via (1) the CR and FX markets, (2) knock-on changes in economic health, and (3) investor portfolio adjustments.

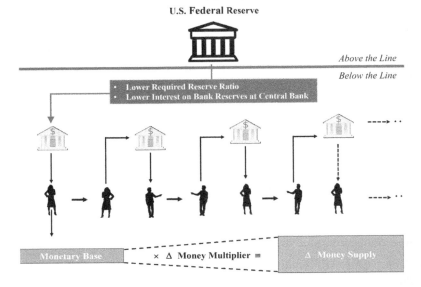

Figure 10.2 Central bank actions that increase the money multiplier.

Transmission via the CR and FX markets

The CR and FX channels of monetary policy might best be explained by separating a central bank's policy tools into those that indirectly affect the FX market (i.e., open market operations, reserve requirement ratio, discount rate, and interest on central bank deposits) from direct central bank intervention in the FX market. We will find that, because the financial markets are so fluid and borderless, the net effects of the indirect and direct tools are the same. Let's see why.

Expansionary monetary policy using tools that indirectly affect the FX market

Suppose a central bank used open market operations, reserve requirement ratio, discount rate, or the interest on central bank deposits to increase the money supply. The increased supply of funds to the CR markets would reduce the real cost of credit, causing C and I to rise, thereby increasing G&S demand (see Figure 10.3 – top portion).

These tools would also have indirect influences on G&S demand via the FX market. An increased supply of funds in Nation A would lower its real cost of credit, which would make the returns on domestic interest-earning

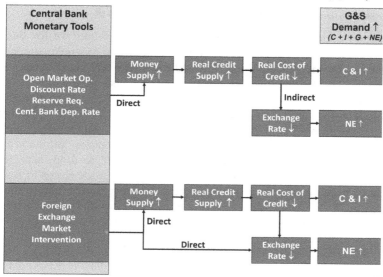

Figure 10.3 Monetary policy channels via the credit and FX markets.

financial assets less attractive relative to foreign-currency-denominated assets. As Nation A's demand for foreign financial assets rose, so would its demand for foreign currencies, causing their values to rise and, therefore, the value of Nation A's currency to fall. Similarly, a falling foreign demand for Nation A's financial assets would decrease the demand for and value of its currency. This depreciation would increase exports, decrease imports, and, therefore, increase Nation A's NE. As NE rose, so would the G&S demand (see Figure 10.3 – top portion).

Expansionary monetary policy using direct FX market intervention

If a central bank intervened directly in the FX market, its actions would simultaneously affect the nation's FX and CR markets. Direct purchases of foreign currency (i.e., sales of the domestic currency) would lower the value of Nation A's currency, which would increase net exports and, therefore, raise G&S demand. The CR market would also be affected because purchases of foreign currency would increase the nation's monetary base and, therefore, raise the supply of real credit. As the supply of real credit increased, its cost would fall, causing C and I to rise, which would increase G&S demand (see Figure 10.3 – bottom portion).

Transmission via knock-on changes in economic health

Monetary policy can cause knock-on changes in household wealth, business profitability, and borrower creditworthiness. For example, suppose expansionary monetary policies lowered a nation's real credit rates and raised RGDP. Falling interest rates would increase household wealth by raising stock, bond, and real estate prices. Greater household wealth would stimulate increases in C. Furthermore, rising RGDP and falling interest rates would improve business cash flows by raising top-line sales, lowering nonoperating costs, and, as a result, increasing profitability. These internally generated cash flows could be used to fund increases in I. Higher stock prices would also encourage new stock issues to fund business expenditures for plant, equipment, and inventories (i.e., to fund increases in I). Finally, higher economic growth rates and lower interest rates would improve borrower creditworthiness, which would increase banks' willingness to lend.

Transmission via investor portfolio adjustments

Figure 10.4 shows a wide variety of assets that investors can hold. These assets compete with each other, based on their relative expected returns. A rising money supply over-weights these portfolios with highly liquid assets, causing investors to use the excess funds to purchase goods, services, and investment assets, such as bonds, stocks, commodities (e.g., precious metals), real estate, and foreign-currency-denominated securities. As a result of these purchases, the prices of investment assets rise, providing investors with capital gains. These capital gains increase investor wealth and reduce the need for them to save, thereby stimulating C and, therefore, G&S demand. Higher G&S demand increases RGDP and lowers the nation's unemployment rate.

The investor-portfolio-adjustment channel helps to explain how central banks can stimulate their economies via *quantitative easing (QE)*, even if the cost of credit approaches, equals, or falls below zero. QE occurs when a central bank floods the market with liquidity by lending and/or purchasing public or private financial assets, such as long-term government bonds, mortgage-backed securities, and private company stocks. Such purchases increase the prices of these financial assets and add liquidity to the financial markets. Investors adjust their portfolios by using the excess funds to purchase real and financial assets. The resulting increase in asset prices, inflation, and expected inflation can stimulate G&S demand, even if interest rates remain unchanged.

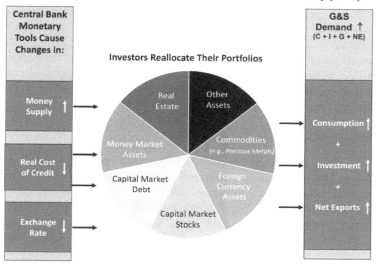

Figure 10.4 Monetary policy channels via investor asset markets.

Bubbles and crashes

Bubbles occur when the prices of financial or real assets rise at unsustainably high rates (i.e., rates that are disconnected from market fundamentals). Stock market and real estate bubbles often start with increases in a nation's money supply, which reduces real credit costs and cause the domestic currency to depreciate. As a result, investors seek higher-yielding, riskier financial and real assets. As the demand for these assets increases, their prices rise. Higher asset prices then become collateral for new loans, which further increase the money supply, reduce real credit costs, depreciate the currency, and lead to subsequent increases in asset prices. Increasingly lower interest returns encourage greater risk taking in order to improve investment results.

If taken to the extreme, underwriting standards begin to deteriorate, resulting in loan officers blindly accepting these higher-priced assets as collateral for new loans and ignoring borrowers' underlying inability to repay their debts. These unsustainable increases in asset prices give the illusion of gains in real (inflation-adjusted) household wealth, thereby raising the demand for luxury products, such as expensive jewelry and exotic vacations, whose demands are also unsustainable.

Money growth stimulates inflation and asset appreciation, which stimulates more borrowing, and, finally, increased borrowing stimulates money growth, which causes higher inflation rates. This self-reinforcing cycle usually comes to an end when the central bank cuts money supply growth rates and asset appreciation moderates or falls. At that point, loans based on expectations of high-and-rising collateral prices turn sour, putting pressure on banks' profitability and solvency. If these losses mount, highly leveraged financial institutions can incur losses that threaten their survival and may also jeopardize the financial system's stability.

Microprudential regulations

Central banks and other financial regulators use microprudential regulations to supervise the activities and risks of *individual* financial institutions. Among the most important are those that address *C*apital (i.e., equity) adequacy, *A*sset quality, *M*anagement quality, *E*arnings, *L*iquidity, and *S*ensitivity to market risks (i.e., the CAMELS rating system). Examples of microprudential policies are limits on bank exposures to any one customer or business sector, controls on maturity and currency risks, caps on customer loan-to-value and debt-to-income ratios, and provisioning requirements for bad loans.

Capital requirements specify the amount of equity that financial institutions must hold to back their risk-adjusted assets. The higher an asset's risk, the more capital the institution must hold. The Bank for International Settlements, which is an organization of international central banks, has taken a leading role in establishing worldwide guidelines for banks' risk-adjusted capital.

Macroprudential regulations

Macroprudential regulations focus on making the *entire* financial system more stable and sound, mainly by reducing or eliminating the impact that one or more failing financial institutions might have on others (i.e., reducing negative externalities). Particular focus is put on ensuring that sufficient liquidity will be present during financial panics, when financial assets are likely to be sold at fire-sale prices and defaults might render healthy borrowers unable to roll over their short-term debts. Catastrophe insurance and bonds that convert to equity during hard times are among the suggested remedies. Two macroprudential tools that have raised special interest are *countercyclical capital requirements* and *forward guidance*.

Countercyclical capital requirements

Countercyclical capital requirements are risk-based equity rules that vary inversely with business cycles. During economic expansions, financial institutions would be required to hold proportionately more capital, thereby slowing credit expansion that could lead to asset bubbles. During contractions, these capital requirements would be reduced, thereby freeing equity that was accumulated during the good times, so that financial institutions could lend to creditworthy customers.

Forward guidance (FG)

Forward guidance (FG) is a central bank tool that promotes financial market stability by transparently communicating future monetary targets to the public. In short, its purpose is to constructively influence market expectations by helping households, businesses, and investors make more rational, predicable, and stable financial and economic decisions. For this reason, public trust and credibility are keys to FG's success.

Central bank's FG commitments have been mainly in the form of promises to keep nominal interest rates low for prolonged periods of time. The duration of these promises can be open-ended, time sensitive, or contingent on one or more economic indicators. For example, in the face of an impending recession, a central bank might pledge to keep the interbank interest rate between 0.00 percent and 0.25 percent "for some time," "for an extended time period," "at least through next year," "the rest of this year," or "for as long as the unemployment rate remains above 6.5 percent and projected medium-term inflation (e.g., one-to-two years ahead) is within 0.5 percent of the central bank's long-term goal of 2 percent."

Conclusion

Monetary policies involve discretionary changes in a nation's money supply, which are caused mainly by central bank tools that affect either the monetary base or money multiplier. The monetary base is affected by open market operations, FX market intervention, and discount rate policies. The money multiplier is affected by changes in reserve requirements and the interest rate banks earn on their reserve deposits at the central bank. Microprudential regulations focus on ensuring the health and soundness of individual financial institutions, and macroprudential regulations focus on the health and soundness of the entire financial system. Monetary policies can be beneficial or harmful, depending on how, when, and where they are used. They affect G&S demand via three major channels, which flow through the (1) CR market, (2) FX market, and (3) investor portfolios.

Notes

1 U.S. dollar checking accounts never leave the country. The former euro holders would now have dollar deposits in U.S. banks and lose their euro deposits in the Euro Area to former U.S. dollar holders.

11 Putting it all together

Let's use what we have learned in Chapters 1 to 10 to analyze how all three macroeconomic markets interact when an economic shock hits one market (or more) and is transmitted to the other two. Figure 11.1 reinforces a major theme in this book, which is the three most important macroeconomic markets move simultaneously, like interconnected gears. Therefore, when one market (gear) moves faster or in a new direction, the others follow in a logical way.

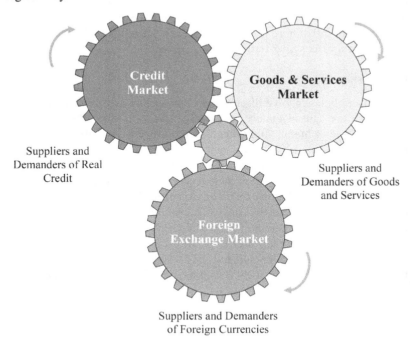

Figure 11.1 Three major macroeconomic markets.

Two examples will help motivate the lessons learned, but any shock could be analyzed using the same tools, reasoning, and techniques. The first example considers the effects of expansionary monetary policy, and the second focuses on expansionary fiscal policy.

The economic effects of expansionary monetary policy

Suppose the European Central Bank (ECB) expanded the European Monetary Union's money supply by lowering bank reserve requirements. What effects would such a policy have on Euro Area's real credit costs, GDP-PI, inflation rate, RGDP, unemployment rate, and exchange rate? Figure 11.2 provides an overall summary of the results.

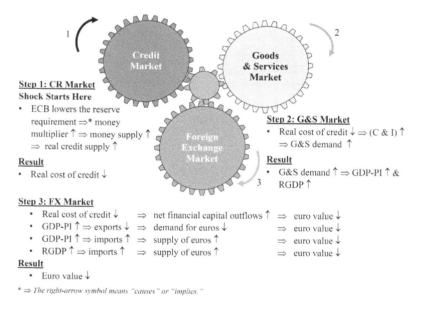

Figure 11.2 Effects of expansionary monetary policy.

CR market

We start our analysis in the CR market, because the central bank's actions increase the nation's money multiplier, which raises its money supply and the supply of real funds to the CR markets. As this supply rises, the Euro-Area's real cost of credit falls, making it cheaper to borrow. Therefore, the amount borrowed per period increases. See Figure 11.3.

Cause	Effects	
Expansionary Monetary Policy	**Real Cost of Credit**	**Quantity of Real Credit per Period**
Supply of Funds to the Euro-Area's Real Credit Market ↑	↓	↑

Figure 11.3 Effects of expansionary monetary policy on the domestic CR market.

G&S market

Reductions in real credit costs are transmitted from the CR market to the G&S market. By lowering the real cost of credit, individuals and businesses borrow and spend more, which increases C and I. Therefore, the nation's G&S demand (i.e., C + I + G + NE) rises (see Figure 11.4). As G&S demand rises, the GDP-PI and RGDP increase. A rising RGDP causes the unemployment rate to fall, and a rising GDP-PI rises puts upward pressure on inflation.

Cause	Effects	
Lower Real Cost of Credit	**GDP-PI**	**RGDP**
(C & I) ↑ ⇒ Euro-Area G&S Demand ↑	↑	↑

Figure 11.4 Effects of a lower real credit cost on G&S demand.

FX market

The FX market is influenced by (1) changes in GDP-PI and RGDP, which are transmitted from the G&S market, and (2) changes in the real cost of credit, which is transmitted from CR market. Let's consider both of these transmission lines.

Transmission from the G&S market to the FX market

A rising GDP-PI reduces the demand for Euro-Area exports and increases the Euro Area's imports from foreign nations. As the demand for euros falls and supply rises, the euro depreciates, and the change in quantity per period is uncertain. See Figure 11.5.

As the Euro Area's RGDP rises, so does its demand for foreign G&S, which increases imports and, therefore, the demand for foreign currencies.

Cause	Effects	
Higher Euro-Area Prices	**Euro Value**	**Quantity of Euros per Period**
Exports ↓ ⇒ Euro Demand ↓	↓	↓
Imports ↑ ⇒ Euro Supply ↑	↓	↑
Net Result	↓	**Uncertain**

Figure 11.5 Effects of higher Euro-Area prices on the euro's value and quantity per period.

As a result, the supply of euros offered to the FX market increases, putting downward pressure on the euro's value. Therefore, the increased RGDP causes the euro's value to fall and quantity per period to rise. See Figure 11.6.

Cause	Effects	
Higher Euro-Area RGDP	**Euro Value**	**Quantity of Euros per Period**
Imports ↑ ⇒ Euro Supply ↑	↓	↑

Figure 11.6 Effects of higher Euro-Area real GDP on the euro's value and quantity per period.

Transmission from the CR market to the FX market

Reductions in the real cost of credit make financial investments in the Euro Area less attractive to foreigners and also make financial investments denominated in foreign currencies, such as U.S. dollars, more attractive to Euro-Area residents. As a result, the falling demand and rising supply of euros in the FX market cause the euro to depreciate. The change in quantity traded per period is uncertain. See Figure 11.7.

Summary

In summary, expansionary monetary policy should cause the Euro-Area's GDP-PI and RGDP to rise, thereby reducing the unemployment rate, putting upward pressure on inflation, and reducing the euro's value.[1] These changes

Cause	*Effects*	
Lower Real Euro Cost of Credit	**Euro Value**	**Quantity of Euros per Period**
Int'l Capital Inflows ↓ ⇒ Euro Demand in FX Market ↓	↓	↓
Int'l Capital Outflows ↑ ⇒ Euro Supply in FX Market ↑	↓	↑
Net Result	↓	**Uncertain**

Figure 11.7 Effects of lower real credit costs on the euro's value and quantity per period

are just first-round effects, because the initial movement of each economic variable ignites changes that reverberate back and forth among the three macroeconomic markets. Nevertheless, the initial changes in macroeconomic variables are the dominant ones. Therefore, the movements explained, so far, indicate the ultimate qualitative direction in which each of these variables moves.

Effect if the European Central Bank intervenes to prevent the euro's depreciation

Suppose the European Central Bank (ECB) did not want the euro to depreciate and intervened in the FX market to prevent its downward movement. Given the circumstances, intervention would seem quite foolish, and here's why. To prevent the euro from falling, the ECB would need to purchase euros in the FX market with its international reserves. In purchasing euros, the ECB would cross our imaginary horizontal line and remove the euro liquidity that it created by lowering the reserve ratio in the first place. Such monetary behavior would be equivalent to throwing armloads of euros out of a 30th-floor window of the ECB in Frankfurt, with the reduction in reserve requirements, and then vacuuming them back in through a tenth-floor window before they hit ground, with FX market intervention.

The economic effects of expansionary fiscal policy

As a second example of how the three macroeconomic markets interact, suppose the Swiss federal government pursued expansionary fiscal policy by increasing government spending on infrastructure projects, such as roads and bridges. What effects should this policy have on Switzerland's real interest rates, GDP-PI, inflation rate, RGDP, unemployment rate, and nominal and real exchange rates? Figure 11.8 provides an overall summary of the results.

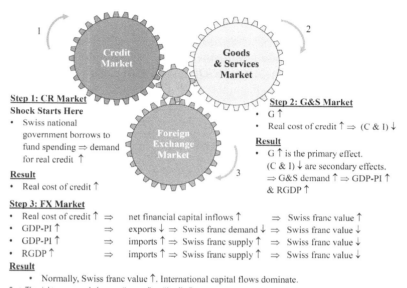

Figure 11.8 Effects of expansionary fiscal policy.

CR market

We start our analysis in the CR market because the Swiss government would need to borrow funds before it could spend them. An increase in the demand for funds would raise Switzerland's real cost of credit and quantity of real credit per period. See Figure 11.9.

Cause	*Effects*	
Expansionary Fiscal Policy	**Swiss Franc Real Cost of Credit**	**Quantity of Real Swiss Franc Credit per Period**
Government Borrowing ↑ ⇒ Demand for Real Credit ↑	↑	↑

Figure 11.9 Effects of expansionary fiscal policy on the CR market.

G&S market

The G&S market would be affected directly by the increase in G and indirectly by the decrease in C and I, caused by rising real borrowing costs.

Direct transmission of G to the G&S market

The increase in G would raise G&S demand, which would cause Switzerland's GDP-PI and RGDP to rise (see Figure 11.10). The nation's unemployment rate would fall, due to the rising RGDP, and upward pressure would be put on the inflation rate due to the higher GDP-PI.

Cause	Effects	
Expansionary Fiscal Policy	**Swiss GDP-PI**	**Swiss RGDP**
G ↑ ⇒ Swiss G&S Demand ↑	↑	↑

Figure 11.10 Direct effects of expansionary fiscal policy on the G&S market.

Indirect transmission from the CR market to the G&S market

Rising real credit costs in Switzerland would cause C and I expenditures to fall. As a result, G&S demand would decrease, causing the GDP-PI and RGDP to fall (see Figure 11.11).

Cause	Effects	
Higher Real Cost of Credit	**Swiss GDP-PI**	**Swiss RGDP**
(C & I) ↓ ⇒ Swiss G&S Demand ↓	↓	↓

Figure 11.11 Indirect effect of CR market adjustments on the G&S market.

Net effect in the G&S market

Conflicting forces in the G&S market may give the impression that the change in GDP-PI and RGDP are uncertain. Due to the rising real cost of credit (i.e., real interest rates), C and I fall, causing G&S demand to decrease. At the same time, increasing G causes G&S demand to rise.

The impact of rising G overpowers the reduction in C and I. We arrive at this conclusion because primary economic effects are stronger than secondary (indirect) effects. The increase in G is direct and unfiltered. By contrast, changes in C and I are secondary and indirect because they are the result of lower real credit costs. Just like ripples on a calm lake after the initial splash of a large rock, these economic waves (i.e., secondary effects) are not as strong as the initial splash (i.e., change in G). See Figure 11.12.

Net Results	*Swiss GDP-PI*	*Swiss RGDP*
G ↑ ⟹ Swiss G&S Demand ↑ *(G ↑ Is the Primary Effect)*	↑	↑
(C & I) ↓ ⟹ Swiss G&S Demand ↓ *(C ↓ & I ↓ Are Secondary Effects)*	↓	↓
Net Change *(Primary Effect > Secondary Effect)*	↑	↑

Figure 11.12 Net effect in the G&S market.

FX market

The FX market is affected by changes in the GDP-PI and RGDP, which are transmitted from the G&S market. It is also affected by changes in real credit costs from the CR market. Let's consider each of these transmission lines.

Transmission from the G&S market to the FX market

Higher prices and rising RGDP change supply and demand forces in the FX market, resulting in the Swiss franc depreciating. Rising prices reduce Swiss exports and increase Swiss imports. As the demand for Swiss francs falls and supply rises, the franc depreciates, but the change in quantity per period is uncertain until the relative strengths of supply and demand changes are known (see Figure 11.13).

Similarly, Switzerland's rising RGDP increases residents' incomes, which raises imports and the supply of Swiss francs to the FX market. As the supply of Swiss francs increases, its international value falls (see Figure 11.14).

Cause	Effects	
Higher GDP-PI	**Swiss Franc Value**	**Swiss Franc Quantity per Period**
Exports ↓ ⇒ Swiss Franc Demand ↓	↓	↓
Imports ↑ ⇒ Swiss Franc Supply ↑	↓	↑
Net Result	↓	**Uncertain**

Figure 11.13 Transmission from the G&S market to the FX market: GDP-PI effects.

Cause	Effects	
Higher RGDP	**Swiss Franc Value**	**Swiss Franc Quantity per Period**
Imports ↑ ⇒ Swiss Franc Supply ↑	↓	↑

Figure 11.14 Transmission from the G&S market to the FX market: RGDP effect.

NET EFFECT FROM THE G&S MARKET TO THE FX MARKET

Increases in the supply of Swiss francs and decreases in demand cause an unequivocal depreciation of the Swiss franc and an uncertain change in the quantity per period.

Transmission from the CR market to the FX market

Higher real credit costs make financial investments in Switzerland more attractive to foreign currency holders and also make financial investments in foreign-denominated currencies, such as U.S. dollars, less attractive to Swiss-franc holders. The rising demand and falling supply in the FX market cause the Swiss franc's value to appreciate, but the change in quantity per period is indeterminate until the relative changes in supply and demand are known (see Figure 11.15).

NET EFFECT FROM THE G&S AND CR MARKETS

Higher real credit costs cause the international value of the Swiss franc to appreciate, but a higher GDP-PI and RGDP cause its value to fall. The

Cause	Effects	
Higher Real Swiss Cost of Credit	**Swiss Franc Value**	**Swiss Franc Quantity per Period**
Int'l Capital Inflows ↑ ⇒ Swiss Franc Demand ↑	↑	↑
Int'l Capital Outflows ↓ ⇒ Swiss Franc Supply ↓	↑	↓
Net Result	↑	**Uncertain**

Figure 11.15 Transmission from the CR market to the FX market.

net effect depends on which of these forces is greater. Under most circumstances (especially in the short run), the international financial markets win this battle. The enormous volume of international financial flows *normally* dwarfs the effects of international product exchanges, causing the Swiss franc's value to rise. Only when there are extreme international financial restrictions, such as exceptionally obstructive exchange controls, would the results be different.

Summary

In summary, expansionary fiscal policy causes Switzerland's real cost of credit, GDP-PI, inflation rate, and RGDP to rise. The nation's unemployment rate falls as RGDP increases, and the value of the Swiss franc appreciates so long as net international financial inflows, due to higher real interest rates, are stronger than net trade-related outflows, due to higher prices and RGDP. Nominal credit costs are sure to rise if the higher GDP-PI also causes expected inflation to rise. Because Switzerland's nominal exchange rate rises, its real exchange rate must rise because the nominal exchange rate (e.g., $/CHF)^2 and GDP-PI increase, thereby reducing Switzerland's price competitiveness in international markets.

These changes are only the first-round effects because movements of each economic variable cause knock-on effects in other markets. Nevertheless, the initial movements in these variables are the dominant ones.

Effect if the Swiss National Bank intervenes to prevent the Swiss franc's appreciation

The Swiss National Bank could prevent the franc from appreciating if it supplied francs to the FX market, which would increase the nation's monetary base and money supply. A larger monetary base would increase Switzerland's money supply, thereby reinforcing the expansionary effects of Switzerland's fiscal policies.

Conclusion

The power of macroeconomics comes from understanding the simultaneous interactions among its three major markets, which are the G&S market, FX market, and CR market. The key is to start in the market impacted by the initial external shock and then extend the analysis to the other two markets.

Notes

1 The change in *real* exchange rate may seem ambiguous because the nominal exchange rate falls and domestic prices rise, but with a few more economic tools, we would see that the real value of the euro must depreciate, which means the falling nominal exchange rate more than offsets rising prices.
2 CHF stands for Confederation Helvetia Franc. "CH" is derived from the Latin name for Switzerland, Confoederatio Helvetica, and "F" is an abbreviation for the franc.

12   Conclusion

The macroeconomic economic concepts and relationships presented in this short book can be used to understand unfolding economic events. They can also be used to decipher what has occurred in the past, but their most valuable use is for future planning. Macroeconomic environments can significantly influence the success or failure of corporate business plans and economy-related legislation. Therefore, creating meaningful strategies and prudent legislation implies competent consideration of possible future economic environments.

Practice makes perfect. Therefore, the next step for anyone who has read and absorbed the contents of this book is to test yourself (often) by critically reading articles in newspapers and magazines, as well as on the Internet. Listen carefully to evening news programs, economic commentaries, and election debates. The more you use these tools and discuss them with others, the sharper your skills and abilities will become. The goal is to turn your understanding of international macroeconomics into an asset that makes valuable contributions to your life – both professionally and personally.

Important to remember are two guiding principles: (1) macroeconomic analyses should focus on the simultaneous movements of the three major markets, and (2) most macroeconomics analyses are conducted or can be improved by using the basic rules of supply and demand. Together, these two principles provide the basis for logical and informed decisions about the effect external shocks can have on a nation's GDP-PI, inflation rate, RGDP and NGDP, unemployment and employment rates, real and nominal credit costs, as well as real and nominal exchange rates. Keeping both of these principles in mind will reduce the chances of jumping to myopic conclusions. They will also keep economics in perspective because, as complex as many economic and financial discussions may seem, most of them are based on logical extensions of economic fundamentals.

Index